T0294253

ILLUSTRATED TALES OF
ESSEX

JOHN WADE

AMBERLEY

First published 2020

Amberley Publishing
The Hill, Stroud
Gloucestershire, GL5 4EP

www.amberley-books.com

Copyright © John Wade, 2020

The right of John Wade to be identified as the Author
of this work has been asserted in accordance with the
Copyrights, Designs and Patents Act 1988.

All rights reserved. No part of this book may be reprinted
or reproduced or utilised in any form or by any electronic,
mechanical or other means, now known or hereafter invented,
including photocopying and recording, or in any information
storage or retrieval system, without the permission in writing
from the Publishers.

British Library Cataloguing in Publication Data.
A catalogue record for this book is available from the British Library.

ISBN 978 1 4456 9878 6 (paperback)
ISBN 978 1 4456 9879 3 (ebook)

Origination by Amberley Publishing.
Printed in Great Britain.

Contents

Introduction

Essex is a place where you learn to expect the unexpected; a county where you can find history and mystery at every turn. It's a place where witches were once reputed to have bewitched people to death, where ghosts are reckoned to roam ancient ruins and where many a resident has had a run-in with the Devil. It's where you find towns and villages with strange names like Ugley, Mucking, Shellow Bowells and Fingringhoe; roads with names like Dancing Dicks Lane, Faggot Yard, Nickerlands, Twitty Fee and Wigley Bush Lane.

Today, the county covers more than 1,400 square miles, and although the distance from Southend-on-Sea, where the Essex coast starts, to Harwich, where it ends, is only a little under 60 miles, the actual shoreline, with all its inlets, creeks, marshes, beaches and even oyster beds, covers more than 350 miles. That makes it the longest coast of any English county. It also boasts the longest pleasure pier in the world, a church partly comprising the oldest wooden building in Europe, the second smallest cathedral in England and a secret yet well-signposted nuclear bunker. Essex is full of ruins that date back to when the county was invaded by the Romans, Vikings, Saxons and Normans. It's where you'll find strange structures and mystery buildings that make no sense until you know their history, lost villages, unknown islands and a wealth of legends, some based on real facts, others no more than stories and rumours passed down through the ages to be exaggerated more with every telling.

Above left: The road to Mucking, one of the stranger place names in Essex.

Above right: The peculiarly named Wigley Bush Lane in Brentwood.

Above left: The marshes at Tollesbury on the River Blackwater that forms one of many inlets along the Essex coast.

Above right: Essex's secret bunker isn't so secret after all, thanks to the proliferation of signs to it.

Dig deep and the county gives up many surprises. Who knew, for example, the part played by Essex in the colonisation of America? Or that a town in Essex was once the capital of England? Did you know that Captain Cook was married in Essex prior to setting out on his voyages of discovery? Or that legend has it that the story of St George slaying a dragon might have begun on Essex soil? Or the significance of the strange word 'Crowstone' found in and around Westcliff? Or even that some of Shakespeare's plays were reputed to have been written by an Essex man?

As a result of the London Government Act of 1963, the 1960s saw parts of Essex absorbed into East London, to become Greater London Boroughs. Even so, because this book is as much about Essex as it once was as it is about the way the county is now, these old Essex towns, irrespective of their current Greater London status, have a place in the pages that follow. Here you'll discover people and places past and present that are a long way distant from the popular perception, generated by reality television shows in recent years, of this sometimes surprising, historically intriguing, often mysterious, but always fascinating English county.

What is a crowstone and why is it so popular in and around Westcliff?

Up the Creek

There has always been something vaguely funny about Barking Creek – not so much the actual place, but rather its name. The Creek was often the butt of music hall humour, and later, in the 1950s when radio comedy was king, it frequently became the punchline to some witticism uttered by a comedian on programmes like *Educating Archie*. Barking Creek is little more than the place where the River Roding enters the River Thames, but that hasn't stopped it playing its part in history and myth.

The Romans were here, as were most other invaders of Ancient Britain. In the poem *The River's Tale*, written by Rudyard Kipling in 1911, in which the poet described British history as witnessed from the viewpoint of the River Thames, he wrote, 'And Norseman and Negro and Gaul and Greek / Drank with the Britons in Barking Creek'.

In the late eighteenth and early nineteenth century, gunpowder was stored at the Creek in brick-built magazines. Ships on their way to fight in foreign wars would leave from London and make their way along the Thames, stopping here to load up with gunpowder, returning later to unload any surplus. The area was considered ideal for the purpose because it was extremely desolate, the only nearby building being an inn called the Crooked Billet. It was also close to water that might be needed to fight fire in the event of an accidental explosion. In 1885, the magazines were sold to the Chilworth Gunpowder Company. Few, if any, of those who live in nearby Chilworth Place will be aware of the significance of their road's name.

There was, however, one thing that, in the nineteenth century, put Barking Creek firmly on the map: sewage.

Chilworth Place, whose name has its origins in the gunpowder industry.

Barking Creek and the Great Stink

Back in early Victorian times, London was a filthy place to live and work with open sewers discharging their waste directly into the River Thames to be washed away briefly, only to return when the tide turned. In 1858, a combination of the hot summer heat and the heavily polluted river resulted in members of parliament hanging sacking soaked with deodorising chemicals at the windows of the House of Commons that bordered the Thames at Westminster. It became known as the year of the Great Stink and resulted in a bill being rushed through parliament that led to the building of a new and far more effective sewage system.

This massively ambitious project saw the construction of underground tunnels which intercepted sewage before it reached the river and, by means of pumping stations and gravity, delivered it to the Thames Estuary, around 14 miles east of London Bridge. Here it was diluted and contained until the start of the ebb tide which flowed the river towards the sea, taking with it the sewage, never to return. Two outfall stations were built in the estuary for that purpose. The southern one was at Erith Marshes in Kent, but the northern one was at Barking Creek.

Tales were told of sewage workers who cultivated fruit and vegetable gardens within the outfall stations, selling their wares to the people of Barking, many of whom enjoyed their succulence until they discovered where they came from.

While it is generally agreed that the expression 'up the creek' might have originated in America in the 1860s, there is another school of thought that believes the creek in the expression and the one at Barking were one and the same. This derivation becomes particularly apposite when considering the particular type of creek usually referred to in the more vulgar version of the expression and the connection of that word with what was being processed at the Barking Creek Northern Outfall.

Barking Creek Northern Outfall in the 1860s.

The Battle of Barking Creek

The Second World War broke out on 3 September 1939. Three days later, following an early morning air-raid alert, a squadron of Hurricanes took off from the Essex airfield in North Weald, followed by two more Hurricanes to act as reserves. In these early days of the war, no enemy aircraft had been seen over Britain, so British pilots would not have known exactly what the enemy looked like. That and poor communications between pilots and base command led to confusion in which the two reserve Hurricanes were mistakenly identified as enemy planes. British spitfires, based at Hornchurch, were ordered into the air to attack.

One pilot successfully ejected; the other, Montague Hulton-Harrop, was killed, making him the first British fighter pilot to be killed in the war, albeit by his own side. He was twenty-six, and is buried with a war grave headstone at St Andrew's Church in North Weald. Two pilots responsible for the death were later court-martialled but were acquitted when it became clear that no blame could be apportioned due to the confusion that prevailed on the day.

Although the event took place over the skies of rural Essex, the skirmish has gone down in history as the Battle of Barking Creek. The reason for this is likely to be because, despite the tragic incident at its heart, the inadequacies of those responsible were considered a bit of a joke – just like Barking Creek.

The grave of Montague Hulton-Harrop, the first British fighter pilot to be killed in the Second World War.

The American cemetery
at St Andrew's Church in
North Weald.

Barking Creek in Ballads and Songs

Rudyard Kipling was not the only person to immortalise Barking Creek in rhyme.
Down through the ages, others have attempted to do the same, some with easily
attributable offerings, others whose origins are now lost in the mists of time.

Paddy Roberts is among those who can be readily identified as the creator of
one such ditty. Born in South Africa, he lived in Devon, where, after a career as
a lawyer and pilot, he began writing songs for popular singers of the 1950s like
David Whitfield, Anne Shelton and Max Bygraves. He also wrote and performed
his own offbeat and quirky songs. In 1960 he turned his thoughts to the delights
of Barking Creek and the kind of person he thought might live there:

> Oh, woe is me, and alas alack!
> A tear rolls down my cheek
> As I tell the story of Nelly Clack,
> The Belle of Barking Creek.

There was also an old music hall monologue by a now forgotten and anonymous
poet of whom nothing is known, although it seems said poet knew the history of
Barking Creek. It begins:

> The Barking Creek bell-ringer's bell it gets rung
> When the fog lies thick on the water,
> Though it's not of the Barking Creek bell my song's sung
> But of the Barking Creek bell-ringer's daughter.
>
> Now she was so lovely, so fair and so squat
> That conductors fell off of their buses
> As she walked down Cable Street bearing on top
> Her bath full of live octopuses.

After some details about how she sells her octopuses the monologue introduces the villain, whom she meets at Barking Creek:

As on the embankment her stock she laid out
In that far from salubrious quarter,
She aroused the wild passions of Algernon Stout
An unemployed Billingsgate porter.

Now Stout was a villain who wallowed in crime
Who lived under some derelict barges
And the day being hot, was laid out on the slime
Where the Barking Creek sewer discharges.

There follows some overlong detail about how Algernon attacks our heroine, loses an eye thanks to a vicious octopus and eventually lays low his victim:

When Algernon spied he was only one-eyed
He was filled with distraught irritation
And grabbed the poor octopus by its inside
As a weapon of flag-e-olation.

The octopus turned inside out with a gulp
As Stout's actions got even distraughter
He sliced them all up and beat to a pulp
The Barking Creek bell-ringer's daughter.

The unknown poet declines to offer any kind of moral to the tale, ending:

But all you bum critics take notice from me
If you're of the feminine gender,
That in Barking today, there's a vacancy
For a lady-like octopus vendor.

The Beginning and End of Creekmouth

Few of those who pass through Barking – and probably a good percentage of those who actually live there – fail to realise that today's urban conurbation is bordered by the River Roding and that Barking has its own town quay. Today, the area is an industrial estate. But back in the early 1800s, Barking was considered to be one of the biggest fishing ports in England, and it was at the town quay that the fishing fleet landed its catch, where it was stored in an enormous ice house. The ice was originally sourced from Norway, but when that proved too expensive, the fishing fleet owners produced their own by flooding the marshland around Barking Creek during the winter and, as the water froze, digging out the ice and storing it in the ice house.

Barking Town Quay today.

Barking Creek as it was in the 1880s.

By the end of the nineteenth century, Barking had ceased to be a fishing port, but by then new industry had begun growing up around the area, and a village was built to house its workers. Among the emerging industries was the Lawes Chemical and Fertiliser Company, and in the 1850s the company's owner, John Bennett Lawes, built a village to primarily house his workers. Close to the Crooked Billet Inn already standing there, the village comprised around fifty houses in two streets, with a school and a mission house. It was called Creekmouth. As well as the chemical factory workers, it also housed people like lightermen who worked the barges on the river. Later, the village housed workers from the new Barking Power Station, built at the location in 1925 to replace an older power station that had been operating since 1897.

It all came to a disastrous end on the night of 31 January 1953 when weather and tides came together in the North Sea to cause a massive surge of water which swept down the east coast of England, flooding towns on the way until it reached the Thames Estuary, from where it raced up the river and totally flooded Creekmouth village. The villagers were made homeless overnight and, despite efforts to try and preserve the buildings, the entire village was subsequently demolished. Where Creekmouth once stood there is now a waste recycling plant. In the mid-1920s, the Crooked Billet was rebuilt close to where the original stood. It is still standing there today.

Creekmouth village front row.

The *Princess Alice* Disaster

In 1878, a pleasure boat on a day trip to the seaside was rammed by a huge coal-carrying ship and sank, killing hundreds of passengers. It happened in the River Thames at Woolwich as the boat was returning to London after a day in Kent. The event is commemorated by a huge mural on a wall in Barking's River Road. Its title is *Soul Searching in Creekmouth* and it shows not only the Princess Alice Disaster, but also the houses of Creekmouth village and the chimneys of Barking Power Station. The disaster is also commemorated by a plaque in open grassland nearby. The mural and the plaque were put in place by the Creekmouth Preservation Society.

Barking Creek Today

These days, what was once largely open marshland is a hive of industrial units. But weave a path through them to the river and you find yourself facing the twin towers of a huge flood barrier. Built over four years and completed in 1983, it stands at the point where the River Roding meets the River Thames. The barrier is 40 meters high, 38 meters wide and weighs nearly 300 tons.

It was built as part of London's flood defence system. Most people know that in times of emergency the Thames Barrier that spans the river between Newham and Greenwich can be lowered. Fewer know of the importance or even the existence of the Barking Creek Barrier that in such circumstances would be lowered before the better-known Barrier further up the river.

Above: Commemorating the *Princess Alice* disaster, a mural in River Road, Barking.

Left: Barking Creek barrier is part of London's flood defence system.

Follies, Towers and Other Curious Buildings

There is a fascination for houses that defy architectural familiarity, as well as for many strange structures that seem to have no useful purpose, other than the simple fact of their existence. Yet each one, strange as it might seem at first sight, has a story to tell. Essex has its share of such curiosities. Here are just a few.

The Essex Taj Mahal

Beside Wrabness village railway station, at the end of a short country lane, there stands a house that is sometimes referred to as the Taj Mahal on the River Stour, which it overlooks across fields. It resembles a cross between a church and a fairy-tale gingerbread house, with a highly ornamental design in four diminishing sections that look as though they could telescope into each other. Its walls are adorned with green and white tiles arranged in symmetrical patterns; its golden

The house at Wrabness, built by artist and poet Grayson Perry.

roof is topped with unusual ornamentation that includes a statue of a naked lady; the windows, which diminish in size with each of the four sections, protrude from the roof in domed dormers; and inside the walls are adorned with brightly coloured tapestries, decorative panelling, ceramics and mosaics.

The house was designed by artist and poet Grayson Perry. It was built as a shrine to a woman called Julie by her second husband. Julie was born on Canvey Island, but later lived in Basildon, Colchester and Wrabness. She was killed when she was knocked down by a scooter driven by a curry delivery driver. At least that's the story. Julie, in fact, didn't die under the wheels of a curry-delivering scooter rider, because she never actually lived. She is a fictional character whose biography was dreamt up by Perry in a long poem, written to provide a social history of Essex since the Second World War.

The Grayson Perry House is one of the most remarkable buildings in this part of Essex. It is available for holiday rentals, but is so popular that prospective holidaymakers are required to enter a ballot for the chance of winning an opportunity to stay there.

Canvey's Dutch Houses

The land that makes up Canvey Island, in the Thames Estuary off the coast of Benfleet, is only a little higher than sea level. Historically, this has meant that the island has always been prone to flooding. But in the seventeenth century, Dutch water engineer Cornelius Vermuyden was called in to make the island safer and more habitable. He did so by draining the land and embanking the island to keep back the sea. The island was home to around 200 Dutch migrants who had fled there seeking refuge from the Duke of Alba. Known as the Butcher of Flanders, he was responsible for carrying out repressive policies in the Netherlands that involved the massacre of thousands of people. The Dutch workers, joined by more of their countrymen, were recruited to carry out Vermuyden's plans.

The Dutch House in Canvey Road on Canvey Island, dating back to the days when Dutch migrants came to Essex.

The workers lived in a small village of houses that they built themselves, following Dutch architectural designs. Today two of the houses still remain intact. One, built in Canvey Road in 1618, has been refurbished and is maintained as a museum. The other, built in 1621 in Haven Road, is privately owned.

Rayleigh's Mystery Cottage

Another cottage with Dutch influences stands at Crown Hill in Raleigh, around 7 miles inland from Canvey. A plaque above the door gives the year 1621, which ties it with the seventeenth-century Dutch migrants to Canvey, but architects and historians who have studied the building place its origins more in the mid-eighteenth century.

In fact, the cottage was probably built in the style of a Dutch building rather than actually by Dutch migrants, as was the case with the similar houses on Canvey Island. It's a single-storey building, eight-sided with a thatched roof. The octagonal shape means it has no real corners – pertinent because superstition in the times when it was built thought evil spirits might hide in corners. Today the cottage is maintained by a charitable trust.

Harlow's Round House

At Latton Street in Old Harlow there once stood a peculiar round house, octagonal in shape with a thatched roof, and reminiscent of the Dutch houses more often seen on or near the Essex coast. It is thought to have been built around 1750, as two dwellings over two floors with two rooms on each. Windows on the upper storey were designed to resemble the petals of flowers. Later, in the twentieth century, it was extended slightly and became a single dwelling.

The Harlow Round House, reminiscent of the Dutch architecture found in other parts of Essex.

Left: Pentlow Tower stands on private land and can only be seen briefly through the trees that surround it.

Above right: Temple of Concord at Audley End.

When the house was built, it stood as a lodge cottage on the approach to Hubbards Hall, a Grade II listed building still standing nearby. The round house was demolished in 1955.

Bull's Tower

The village of Pentlow lies close to the town of Braintree. It was here, in 1859, that the Revd Edward Bull decided to erect a memorial to his parents, and he did so in the garden of what was then the rectory. But this was no ordinary memorial. It was – and still is – a tall, slim brick-built tower standing 95 feet high. Also known as the Pentlow Tower, the edifice is built of red brick with black designs and includes windows on three floors. Inside, 114 steps of a spiral staircase lead to the top. At the time the tower was built it is said that the view from the top encompassed forty-one churches, sixty windmills and a couple of castles.

Temple of Concord

The gardens of a stately home on the outskirts of Saffron Walden are the unexpected location of a Corinthian temple. Looking like a Greek temple in the midst of very English landscaped gardens, the imitation ruin is at Audley End, one of the finest Jacobean country houses in England. The design of its grounds, while influenced by many landscape gardeners over the years, are largely the work of Lancelot 'Capability' Brown and Robert Adam, whose work was commissioned in the eighteenth century. In 1790, at the instigation of Sir John Griffin, the then incumbent of Audley End, English architect Robert Furze Brettingham was commissioned to design the folly. It's rectangular in shape, dominated by unfluted

Corinthian columns and standing on a raised mound known as a ha-ha. It was erected in celebration of King George III's recovery from madness – somewhat prematurely as it turned out.

Jumbo Water Tower

In Colchester, in the late 1800s, water was in short supply, both clean enough for drinking and in sufficient quantities for firefighting. The Waterworks Company, located in the town, supplied clean water, but only to wealthy customers and for no more than a few hours a day. With the passing of the Public Health Act in 1875, however, Colchester Council adopted an ambitious plan to clean up the town's water supply. The council bought the Waterworks Company and proposed the building of an enormous water tower that would supply clean drinking water, and water for fighting fires, to the whole of the town twenty-four hours a day. With a tank capacity of 221,000 gallons and standing more than 130 feet high, it used more than a million bricks and cost £11,000 to build.

The tower gained its nickname from the Revd John Irvine, whose rectory was a mere 16 feet from the place where the tower was to have been originally built. Decrying the plans in letters to the press, he called it a Jumbo because of its size and in reference to Jumbo the Elephant, a famous occupant of London Zoo at the time.

His objections fell on deaf ears, and the council went ahead and built the tower, albeit 60 feet further away from the rectory than had previously been planned. To add insult to injury, however, the tower was topped by a gilded weathervane shaped like an elephant.

Colchester's Jumbo Water Tower.

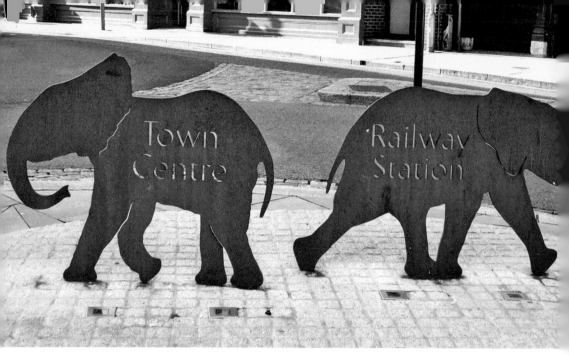

The elephant theme continues in the town's street signs.

The tower was opened in 1883, but soon proved to be somewhat unfit for purpose. It transpired that it wasn't strong enough to support a full tank of water, and could only supply water to the inhabitants of Colchester for six hours a day. Then, when a fire broke out the year the tower opened, it took longer to get water to the blaze than had been the case before the tower was built. Despite further problems, including a crack that appeared in the tower following the Essex earthquake in 1884, the tower remained in use until 1984, and still stands today as a public attraction near Colchester's Balkern Gate. Meanwhile, in modern-day Colchester, the jumbo theme continues with elephant-shaped signposts in the high street.

Epping Water Tower

In the mid-nineteenth century, deaths from typhoid and cholera reached crisis point in the town of Epping. After nearly twenty years of campaigning, Dr Joseph Clegg, a local general practitioner, was finally granted a water tower for the town. It was built for the Epping Rural Sanitary Authority in 1872.

Built with red brick in a Victorian Gothic style, it stands 90 feet high. The door at the base and the windows above are almost church-like in their styles, two side-by-side halfway up the tower and one above, under arches of blue and grey brick.

In recent years, Dr Clegg has been honoured with a blue plaque on the side of the tower that stands today in Epping High Street.

Left: Epping Water Tower, the inspiration of Dr Joseph Clegg.

Above right: A blue plaque on the side of Epping Water Tower honours the work of Dr Clegg.

Hockley Pump Room

Essex is not a county known for its spas. But in the nineteenth century, a pump room was opened in the town of Hockley that was said to be comparable to those found in the more famous spa towns of Bath in Somerset and Royal Tunbridge Wells in Kent.

Its opening was instigated when a husband and wife who had moved to Hockley from Cheltenham dug a well in their back garden and discovered a spring of what appeared to be health-giving water. It was later found that the water contained a high percentage of sodium chloride (salt), as well as calcium and magnesium derived from the clay of London, through which the water from the spring had passed.

Hockley Pump Room was once a famous Essex spa.

With the help of a local businessman, an architect was employed and a magnificent pumping room was built, opening for business in 1843. To support it, a hotel and villas were added for health-seeking visitors. People flocked to Hockley and the water was even sent to London to be bottled and distributed abroad. It was claimed that the water could cure asthma and indigestion, as well as liver, kidney and bladder infections. For a while, business boomed. Then, five years after the pump house opened, fewer people began to make the journey to Hockley to take the waters. As the public failed to come, the spa faded away.

Today, the fine old pump house still stands. Following the decline in its popularity as a spa it variously became used as a Baptist chapel, billiard hall and clothing factory. It stands today, privately owned, in Hockley's Main Road.

Bateman's Tower

Standing at the entrance to the River Colne at Promenade Way in Brightlingsea there is a short tower which, since it leans slightly to one side, looks a little like a crooked lighthouse. The story goes that it was intended to be just that when there were plans to turn the area into a major port, but it was abandoned when the plans failed to materialize. In fact, it's much more likely that the tower is a folly,

Above left: Bateman's Tower at Brightlingsea has had a mixed past.

Above right: Layer Marney Tower is the tallest Tudor gatehouse in the country.

built in 1883 by John Bateman, a local man, as a place where his daughter could take the sea air to help her recuperate from consumption. During the Second World War, the roof was removed so that the members of the Royal Observer Corps could use it as an observation post. It was restored to its original condition in 2005, thanks to a donation from the Heritage Lottery Fund. The tower is used today by local sailing organisations to help administer races.

Layer Marney Tower

In 1520, Lord Henry Marney, a friend of King Henry VIII, began work on building a grand country residence with the tallest gatehouse in Britain. Unfortunately, Lord Marney died in 1523, and his son John, who continued the building work, died two years later, leaving no heir to complete the project. So the house was never finished, but the tower still stands in the village of Layer Marney, where it retains its status as the tallest Tudor gatehouse in the country. With ninety-nine steps covering eight floors, it was designed with double windows to give the impression of even more floors. It is built of red brick with black glazed bricks for decoration. Today it is a popular venue for weddings and has featured as the backdrop in several television series.

Southend Crowstone

The point where the River Thames becomes the North Sea isn't easy to define without some kind of marker to indicate the exact position. That's the purpose of this somewhat unassuming obelisk. Although known as the Southend Crowstone, it is actually on the beach at Chalkwell, close to Westcliff-on-Sea. An invisible boundary between this and a second obelisk across the estuary on the Isle of Grain in Kent marks the spot where river becomes sea, and vice versa. The origins of the word crowstone in this context are unknown, although the word is usually defined as being the top stone of the gable end of a house. The Southend Crowstone has had several incarnations over the centuries. The current version was erected in the 1950s to replace an eighteenth-century square granite pillar which was moved to nearby Priory Park.

Mersea's Wheel Tomb

There is a road on Mersea Island called Pharos Lane. The name is not, as some have suggested, a mis-spelling of Pharaoh and even if it was, there is no connection between this area of Essex and any ancient Egyptian monarchs. Pharos is, in fact, another word for a lighthouse (as in the Pharos or Lighthouse of Alexandria, one of the Seven Wonders of the Ancient World). The lane is named after Roman remains found nearby when the foundations of a large circular structure were excavated in 1897 and originally thought to be the foundations of a Roman

Left: The Southend Crowstone marks the spot where the River Thames becomes the North Sea.

Above right: The ancient wheel tomb at Mersea.

lighthouse. Some years later, it was discovered that this was actually a rare Roman wheel tomb.

The tomb took the form of a small hexagonal chamber from which six walls extended out to a 3-foot-thick encircling wall, then another 4 feet to an outer wall. The entire structure measured 65 feet in diameter. It is thought that this type of tomb was built as a mausoleum for an important Roman family. Similar wheel tombs have been discovered in Germany, Italy and, in Britain, in Kent. The Mersea tomb no longer exists as it was destroyed by building works in the 1960s.

Ilford Castle

In 1765, Charles Raymond, a retired sea captain who had made a fortune in the East India Company, came to Essex and built a small castle. It was triangular in shape with a tower at each corner. Its purpose was to provide a huge mausoleum for himself and his family, but it also came to be used as a banqueting house. The mini-castle cost £420 to build and became known in the area as Raymond's Folly, although the names that have come down through the years are Ilford Castle and Cranbrook Castle, the latter named after the area where it was built, now part of the London Borough of Redbridge. Captain Raymond died in 1788. He and his wife Sarah were not buried in the castle mausoleum, but in the neighbouring town of Barking. The castle was demolished in 1923 to make way for a tennis club.

Ilford Castle before it was demolished in 1923.

Harwich Treadwheel Crane

On Harwich Green, close to the seafront, there is what appears to be a large wooden hut with the jib of a crane protruding from its side. It is a crane, but what makes it unusual is its motive power. Built in 1667, the crane was operated by two men walking around a large treadmill inside the hut. In the seventeenth century Harwich was known for its shipbuilding and the man-powered crane was originally used in that industry for lifting heavy loads. Its design is unique to Britain. Remarkably, the crane was in use as late as 1928, when the shipyard closed and the crane was transferred to its current resting place where it has become a tourist attraction.

Barking's Fake Ruins

Proof that follies don't have to be ancient can be found in one that stands in a side street of Barking. It's close to where Barking Abbey was built back in the seventh century and some believe it to be a part of that original building. Closer examination, however, reveals a wall far higher than any of the actual nearby existing ruins with a short staircase leading up to a bricked-up doorway, a series of recesses, some statues, a second closed-off doorway, what might or might not have been a chimney and even a stone goat at the very top. In actuality, this is a modern folly, built purely as a piece of art by apprentice bricklayers in 2007, using old bricks, to recreate what is meant to represent a fragment of Barking's lost history.

Above left: Harwich treadmill crane, a design unique to Britain.

Above right: Fake ruins in Barking, built in 2007 by apprentice bricklayers.

Witch-hunting in Essex

Essex was the first county in England to execute a woman for being a witch. Agnes Waterhouse was placed on trial at Chelmsford Assize, accused of causing illness to several people, using sorcery to kill livestock and even bringing about the death of her husband. She was hanged at Chelmsford in 1566.

Although England's first Act against witchcraft was passed in 1542, it was soon repealed before too many innocent people were falsely accused of the crime. Twenty years later, in 1562, a new Act was passed, resulting in the accusations of a great many alleged witches, including Agnes Waterhouse. Witchcraft laws were abolished in England in 1736, but not before England's most notorious witch hunt had been perpetrated by the man who called himself The Witchfinder General.

Matthew Hopkins

Tucked away in the north-west corner of Essex, standing on Holbrook Bay, which is part of the River Stour, lies Manningtree, whose name is thought to be derived from Many Trees. A sign on the outskirts of the town, welcoming visitors to the area, shows a mixture of pictures of local scenes, and a single person, a man in seventeenth-century dress including high boots, cloak and tall hat. This was one of the Manningtree's most infamous residents: Matthew Hopkins, self-proclaimed Witchfinder General.

Above left: The town sign for Manningtree in North Essex.

Above right: Matthew Hopkins, who called himself Witchfinder General.

The English Civil War, which waged between 1642 and 1651, was a time of unease, religious rivalry, superstition and paranoia, a climate of which Hopkins took full advantage. Born in Suffolk, the son of a Puritan clergyman, Hopkins was a religious zealot, of whom little was known until the early 1640s when he moved to Manningtree. It was here that it was claimed he overhead some women of the town discussing their meetings with the Devil. Along with his associates, he moved in and brought them to trial. As a result of his actions, twenty-three women were tried at Chelmsford in 1645. Four died in prison, the rest were found guilty of witchcraft and hanged.

Appointing himself the title of Witchfinder General, which he falsely claimed had been authorised by parliament, Hopkins and his associates rampaged through the towns and countryside of East Anglia, charging for their services as they searched out witches. Innocent women accused of the crime were deprived of sleep until they confessed. Various methods of proof were also instigated. Victims were pricked with needles to see if they bled, and if they didn't they were proclaimed to be witches. Women were tied up and thrown into a river or other water and if they floated they were witches, if they sank (and often drowned) they were innocent. Their bodies were searched for marks of the Devil, which were said to be devoid of feeling and unable to bleed. If no such marks were found, they were sometimes produced by pricking. Basically, from the moment any woman was accused of being a witch, she was doomed.

Hopkins wrote a book on his methods of hunting witches, their trials and executions. He died at his home in Manningtree in 1647, probably of tuberculosis. It has been estimated that around 500 women were found guilty of witchcraft and executed during these times, of which Hopkins and his associates were responsible for around 300.

Stories of Essex witches, however, were told before the arrival of Matthew Hopkins, and for centuries after his demise. Here are a few of them.

A plaque on the side of The Cage, a medieval prison in St Osyth where witches were kept before being hanged.

The Witches of Canewdon

In the sixteenth century the mudflats and marshes of Essex that lay close to and south of the River Crouch were desolate places, bleak and isolated. Maybe that's why Matthew Hopkins never made it to Canewdon, which before, during and after his reign of terror, was known for being a place where witches gathered. Legend had it that the village would always contain six witches, three from the lower classes and three from the upper classes. It was probably one of the last places where witches were still believed to exist, even as late as the end of the nineteenth century. Stories abounded about Canewdon residents who could bewitch wagon wheels and bicycle tyres, inflict people with lice or do no more than stand in the churchyard with glaring eyes aimed at parishioners on their way to worship in a church that was renowned for witches dancing among the gravestones.

Two members of the Canewdon community were tried as witches between 1580 and 1590. One was accused of bewitching to death a twelve-month-old child and, although acquitted at her trial, died in jail before she could be released. A second was committed to five years in jail for practising witchcraft. When it was clear she did not mean to repent on her release, she was excommunicated, which many believed damned the soul to hell.

Canewdon was also the location for a contest between two witches, the victor being James Murrell, a shoemaker from nearby Hadleigh who began business there in 1812. Known as a master of witches, he used his powers for good, curing the sick by conjuring up good spirits and angels to fight bad spirits that were troubling local residents. The Canewdon witching contest involved Murrell commanding another witch to die, which she did, on the spot. There were also stories about Murrell offering to force other witches to confess their deeds by having them dance around the Canewdon churchyard. Evidently the vicar refused to allow this in case it proved that his own wife was a witch.

Canewdon Church, where witches were once thought to dance among the gravestones.

George Pickingill, who lived in Canewdon in the 1860s, was thought to have sold his soul to the Devil, even though he used his witchcraft for good as well as evil. On the good side, he provided herbal remedies for the sick and was adept at finding lost objects. On the bad side, it was reckoned that he could curse people so that they fell sick and could only be cured by his touch. It was claimed that he set up and controlled nine covens of witches in Essex and surrounding counties.

Canewdon Church also has its fair share or bewitching connections. Legend has it that if a stone falls from the church's tower, a witch will die. Walk around the church at midnight and witches are said to appear before you. Halloween is the most notorious time for such excursions when, running around the church in an anti-clockwise direction will force the Devil to appear. Running forwards or running backwards and the number of tours taken around the tower are said to release all kinds of supernatural phenomena, so much so that even today, police have been known to barricade the area at Halloween to prevent too many visitors from racing around the church at midnight.

The Woman Who Controlled the Weather

At Leigh-on-Sea, close to the mouth of the Thames Estuary where the river meets the North Sea, there is a pub called the Sarah Moore. It's named after a local woman of the nineteenth century reputed to be a witch who could control the weather.

According to legend, Sarah would sit on the quay where she claimed to be able to sell sailors good weather. For the price of a penny, she would provide a sailor about to go to sea with a piece of knotted string, into which she had tied

The Sarah Moore pub in Leigh is named after a local woman reputed to be a witch.

the wind. Once out to sea, the sailor would untie the string. One knot brought a gentle breeze, two would result in a strong wind and three would bring a storm.

One day a foreign ship arrived at Leigh and its captain, hearing of Sarah's claims, forbade his crew to have anything to do with her. When she heard this, she took her revenge by throwing a great storm at the ship as it left for the open sea. The crew tried to lower the sails but were prevented by rigging that became tangled with the mast. Eventually, the captain felled the mast with three strokes of an axe, at which point the storm abated. When the crew got the stricken ship back to land, they found Sarah dead on the quayside, killed by three strokes of an axe.

In fact, there was a great storm recorded in this area around that time, but it happened in 1870, three years after Sarah's rather more natural death in 1867.

A Grave with a Cage

In the graveyard at St Edmund's Church in East Mersea there is a grave covered by an iron cage. An inscription on the grave reveals that it is the resting place of Sarah Wrench who died on 6 May 1848, aged fifteen years and five months. The reasons why her grave is covered by a cage are somewhat mysterious.

A popular theory from local folklore is that Sarah was a witch and the cage was placed over her grave because people were so scared of her that they meant to prevent her from escaping after death and rejoining the land of the living. A more likely explanation is that she was disgraced in some way, probably because she had an illegitimate child, or maybe committed suicide. Supporting this theory is the fact that she is buried on the north side of the church, which was unconsecrated ground.

Cages such as this one were known as mortsafes and were placed in position to prevent grave robbers exhuming the body. The usual purpose of these resurrection men, as they were also called, was to get a body that could be sold for medical research. The mortsafe that covers Sarah's grave, however, is more likely to have been put in place to prevent local inhabitants desecrating the grave of a disgraced girl, who might or might not have been a witch.

The Felsted Hag

In the village of Felsted, there is a restaurant built into an old timber house that dates back to 1596. The builder was George Boote and he was so proud of it that he had his name carved into the side of the building. A more modern sign hanging from the front of the building identifies it as Boote House. What makes the building particularly unusual, however, is a rather gruesome gargoyle-like carving of a naked and shackled woman that adorns one corner under the overhanging first floor.

Some say that it's an effigy of George Boote's wife, whom he married out of pity after a witch cursed her with ugliness. But, since the woman in the carving has cloven feat, it is more likely that it depicts Alice Alberta, Felsted's only convicted

Above: Boote House restaurant in Felsted.

Left: The Felsted hag who might have been Felsted's only witch.

witch. In 1593, Alice was tried and convicted at the Essex Assize in Chelmsford, accused of bewitching twenty-two sheep worth £5, a cow worth 40 shillings (£2), a calf and a pig, each worth 8 shillings (40p). She pleaded not guilty, but was found guilty and hanged for her alleged crimes.

Today, at Halloween, it is said the carving comes to life and is seen running around the streets of the town.

The Bells Beneath the Water

If you happen to be on the banks of the River Crouch on a stormy night and you hear ghostly bells tolling from under the water, it could all be down to one member of a whole family of witches who lived in the area in the early 1800s. Among them was Harriet Hart who, it is said, suffered from an allergy brought on by church bells. She was particularly allergic to the bells of the church in her village of Latchingdon, so one night she stole them. Taking the bells to nearby Burnham-on-Crouch, she planned to transport them to the opposite bank of the river. One story says she meant to dump them there, another says her plan was to meet up with a second witch so they could use the bells in their witchcraft. She was, however, foiled in both pursuits because, failing to find a boat for her purposes, she used a barrel with a feather for an ore. Needless to say, neither she nor the bells survived the crossing and they sunk into the river – where some say the bells can still be heard from beneath the surface on stormy nights.

Another story about others of the Hart family who lived in nearby Fambridge concerned a husband and wife, accused of being witches, being tied to a boat by a rope and pulled through the water. Mr Hart sank and came close to drowning, which proved he was innocent, whereas Mrs Hart floated, which proved to all that she was a witch.

Although the Act repealing the laws against witchcraft was passed by parliament in 1736, fines or imprisonment could still be imposed on those who claimed to be able to use magical powers. That Act was only repealed in 1951.

The desolate marshes at Fambridge, an area once famous for stories of witchcraft.

The First Capital of Britain

Colchester is Britain oldest recorded town and, for a while in Roman times, it was the country's capital. It began as an Iron Age settlement that became known as Camulodunum. When the Romans invaded England in AD 43 they saw the location of the town as one of strategic importance and built a fortress close to the original tribal centre. Within the fort an area was built for retired Roman soldiers and this became Britain's first city. It was destroyed by Queen Boudicca in AD 60, but subsequently rebuilt by the Romans. When the Romans left, the Saxons moved in. Later, when William the Conqueror needed a power base in England, he built a castle here on top of a former Roman temple in 1076.

There are several theories as to how Colchester got its name. Being situated on the River Colne, one theory is that the name was derived from Colne Castra. Another theory is that the name is derived from the Latin word Colonia, a type of Roman settlement. The earliest forms of today's name date to the tenth century when the area was known as Coleneaster or Colneceastre. The name Colchester was first known in the fifteenth century. Today, Colchester abounds in history and historic landmarks, many of them in and around the town centre, that give indications of its rich and colourful past.

Colchester Castle has had a long and varied history.

Colchester Castle

William the Conqueror's castle was designed by the Bishop of Rochester, who was also responsible for the White Tower in the Tower of London. The castle has had a varied history. It was captured by King John's rebellious barons in 1199 and recaptured by the king in 1215. In the fourteenth century its dungeons were converted into prison cells and it served as a jail and prison for many years more. In the seventeenth century, it was where Witchfinder General Matthew Hopkins carried out his investigations. It also played a role in the English Civil War. By the end of the seventeenth century, the castle had fallen into disrepair, but was restored by lawyer Charles Gray, who created parkland around it. When Gray died the castle was sold to the Corporation of Colchester. Today it still stands in the centre of parkland and operates as a museum.

Roman Walls and Gateways

When the Romans rebuilt Colchester after the attack by Queen Boudicca, they encircled the town with high defensive stone walls with just five gateways. The best of these that can still be seen today is Balkerne Gate, the main entrance to the town in Roman times and today the oldest surviving Roman gateway in Britain. In Roman times it consisted of two large arches with smaller openings for pedestrians each side. Standing alone today, it would originally have been incorporated into the wall that surrounded the town.

The area around the Balkerne Gate also features the Jumbo Water Tower and the Hole in the Wall Inn, a seventeenth-century pub which straddles part of the Roman wall remains. It was built after the Siege of Colchester.

Balkerne Gate, once part of the Roman wall that surrounded Colchester.

Colchester's Dutch Quarter

In the sixteenth century, Flemish protestant refugees, fleeing persecution after their rebellion against Catholic Spain had been defeated, came to the east coast of England and settled in Colchester in what today is known as the Dutch Quarter. The area is close to Colchester High Street, spanning several roads of timber-framed houses built in the Dutch style.

On the wall of one house is a plaque erected by the Corporation of Colchester in memory of Jane and Ann Taylor who lived there between 1796 and 1811. According to the plaque, they were the 'authors of *Original Poems for Infant Minds*'. Their most famous English nursery rhyme was *Twinkle Twinkle Little Star.*

The Dutch Quarter also contains St Martin's Church, parts of which date back to the eleventh century, although most of it dates to the fourteenth century, before the arrival of the refugees. The walls incorporate Roman bricks. Its tower was never rebuilt after being damaged during the English Civil War. Today the church is redundant and has been so since 1953, but it is open most days and can be visited to admire the medieval architecture.

St Helen's Chapel can also be found in the Dutch Quarter. It dates back to Saxon times, possibly the eighth century, although the first record of its name is in 1097. The church's ancestry, however, goes back even further, since it was built on the foundations of a Roman temple, whose remains can still be seen at the base of the chapel's walls. Today the chapel is used as a Greek Orthodox church.

The Dutch Quarter, close to Colchester High Street.

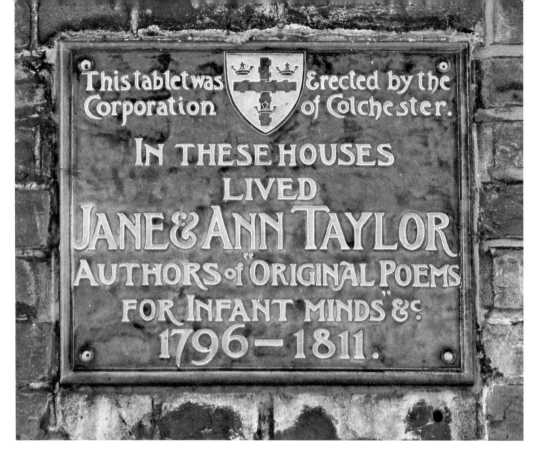

Above: A plaque on a house in Colchester's Dutch Quarter celebrates the writer of *Twinkle Twinkle Little Star*.

Below right: Parts of St Martin's Church date back to the eleventh century.

St Helen's Chapel dates back to Saxon times.

St Botolph's Priory

In the heart of modern Colchester stand the remains of St Botolph's Priory, Britain's first Augustinian monastery, dating back to 1099. All that remains today is the nave of the priory church, which was mostly built with brick and stone from the old Roman city. The ruins are notable for their Romanesque architecture, impressive columns, rounded arches and ornamentation. The priory was dissolved by King Henry VIII in 1536 and badly damaged during the English Civil War during the Siege of Colchester in 1648. Today, it's still possible to see damage to the walls caused by Royalist cannons at that time.

All that remains of St Botolph's Priory, Britain's first Augustinian monastery.

The square tower of Holy Trinity Church dates back to 1050.

Holy Trinity Church

Holy Trinity Church is dominated by its square Saxon tower which dates back to *c.* 1050, although the main body of the church attached to tower was built 300 years later. In the churchyard lies the grave of William Gilberd, physician to Queen Elizabeth I. Inside, many medieval items remain, including a sixteenth-century font, seventeenth-century coats of arms and painted carved heads in the nave.

The church is no longer used for worship. It was made redundant in 1956, and today is used as an arts centre and café.

The Colchester Earthquake

According to records kept by the British Geological Society, Colchester has had more reported earthquakes than anywhere else in Britain, dating back to 1048. The biggest of these happened on 22 April 1884, at 9.18 in the morning, when Britain was hit by the country's most destructive earthquake ever. It lasted twenty seconds and measured 4.6 on the Richter scale. Although usually referred to as the Colchester Earthquake, because of the damage inflicted on the town, it also affected a good deal of the surrounding villages.

Above left: The spire of Lion's Walk Church that was toppled in the Colchester Earthquake.

Above right: A plaque on side of Lion's Walk Church's spire commemorates the earthquake.

At Colchester's Lion Walk Congregational Church, incongruously situated in the middle of a modern shopping precinct, the top of the spire became detached, crashing to the ground, and the Roman Catholic Church in Priory Street was also damaged, along with more than 1,200 other buildings in the area. A pub in Old Heath was destroyed, windows were blown out of train carriages at North Station and it was reported that the train driver was thrown from his cab. It was reckoned that the earthquake was felt as far away as Devon and Ostend in Belgium.

For many years the Colchester Earthquake went unremembered. But in 2016, a plaque was placed in the pavement outside St Peter's Church near Colchester High Street to commemorate the event. In 2019, another plaque was unveiled on the side of what is now Lion Walk United Reformed Church to also commemorate Britain's biggest earthquake.

How *The Graphic*, a weekly illustrated newspaper, reported the earthquake in May 1884.

Seeing the Light

Traditionally, lighthouses are situated in the sea at locations considered dangerous to shipping navigation. Conventionally they take the form of tall towers, usually but not always with revolving lights at the top to warn ships and boats in the area to keep clear of hazards beneath the surface. Many Essex lighthouses were originally built on land, one even in the middle of a town, and some lights were situated neither on land nor in the sea, but aboard ships. While some of the county's lighthouses have now been demolished, others still stand, though many are no longer used for their original purpose. Lighthouses in Britain were, and are still, overseen by Trinity House, a charity dedicated to the safeguard of ships and their sailors. The charity is responsible for the General Lighthouse Authority for England, Wales, the Channel Islands and Gibraltar.

Harwich High and Low Lights

Harwich, in North Essex, boasts two lighthouses, one standing in the centre of the town, the other 150 yards away on the coastal path. Originally they were made of wood and, at that time, featured in a painting by John Constable, first exhibited in the 1820s. The painting can be seen in London's Tate Gallery. In 1818, the wooden structures were demolished and replaced by brick-built versions. They are known as the Harwich high and low lights.

Harwich high light stands in the centre of the town.

Harwich low light is situated on the coast.

The high light, which stands in the town, is 90 feet tall; the nearby low light is only half that size, so that its light shines out beneath the one at the top of the high light. They were built to enable sailors to navigate the shallow waters of the area. When vessels were positioned so that one light was seen directly above the other, they were on course for a safe passage.

Today, the high light is open to the public and anyone brave enough to ascend its 100 steps to take in the magnificent view from the top. It is used as an exhibition venue. The low light houses a maritime museum.

Dovercourt High and Low Lights

In 1863, the sea currents shifted, rendering the two Harwich lighthouses redundant and resulting in them being decommissioned. In their place, two new structures, still standing and recently restored, were built to serve a similar purpose nearby at Dovercourt. One stands on the shore, the other some way out to sea, linked at low tide by a causeway. Made of cast iron with iron legs and an outside staircase leading up to the living quarters and light, these are less aesthetically attractive than their Harwich counterparts, but were built to serve a similar purpose, guiding sailors safely to port with their high and low lights.

Both Dovercourt lighthouses were decommissioned in 1917, after which they fell into disrepair. They were restored in 1988.

Chapman Lighthouse

At the mouth of the Thames Estuary, close to Canvey Island, mudflats at one time posed a serious threat to ships that, having sailed across the North Sea, needed to enter the estuary and head up the River Thames to London. To warn sailors of the dangerous shallow waters, Chapman Lighthouse was erected in 1849.

It was designed at Trinity House, and took the form of an iron lattice structure, built on seven piles screwed into the bed of the river by means of a bladed screw on the foot of each pile. Living quarters were built on the top of the piles and a

Above left: Dovercourt high and low lights.

Above right: Chapman lighthouse before its demolition in 1957.

light tower was added to the top of that. The complete structure stood 74 feet tall and its light could be seen for 11 miles. A fog warning bell was fixed to the seaward side of the lantern housing for use when weather conditions might obscure the light.

At low tide, the keepers could wade or even walk the half mile from the shore to the lighthouse across the mudflats. At high tide, a rowing boat, suspended from spigots on the side of the lighthouse, was lowered to enable them to make the journey.

During the First and Second World Wars, the lighthouse became a meeting point for convoys leaving the Thames Estuary for the open sea. Corroding ironwork eventually led to Chapman Lighthouse being decommissioned and demolition began in 1957. A bell buoy now marks the spot where the lighthouse once stood 800 yards off the coast of Canvey.

Naze Tower

In 1721, before lighthouses were commonplace, Trinity House built a huge 86-foot, eight-sided tower on the Naze, the headland above the town of what is now Walton-on-the-Naze. It is believed to be the only one of its type in the world. At one time, with a light at the very top, the tower was used as a marker for ships as they approached the harbour at nearby Harwich.

The Naze Tower was a very early form of lighthouse.

Inside, a spiral staircase leads to eight floors which today contain exhibitions, an art gallery and museum, with the chance for members of the public to take in some of the most stunning views of the Essex coast from a viewing platform at the very top. Tragically, the tower might soon be lost to coastal erosion, as every year a significant part of the Naze falls into the sea, effectively moving the tower closer to the edge of the cliffs with every fall.

Gunfleet Lighthouse

Six miles off the coast of Frinton-on-Sea, Gunfleet Lighthouse, constructed in 1850 and similar in design to those at Dovercourt, still stands. Mounted on seven piles screwed into the seabed, it houses living quarters with a light tower on top. When it was active, the beam from its light, revolving every thirty seconds, was visible for 10 miles as a warning to sailors of the treacherous sands around this coastline.

Gunfleet lighthouse was deactivated in 1921, but in 1974 there was an attempt to occupy it and turn it into a pirate radio station that would have been called Radio Atlantis, had the authorities not put a stop to it. The lighthouse is still in use today as an automated weather station.

Stone Ness lighthouse.

Stone Ness Lighthouse

Lighthouses are not always situated in, or close to, the sea. Some are distributed along the banks of the River Thames between London Bridge and the estuary, as the river passes through Essex. This one is placed on the Essex bank between Grays and Purfleet, close to where the M25 motorway crosses the river. Standing 44 feet high, it was established in 1885 and today carries a wind generator on its top to run a light that is visible for 9 miles.

Lightships

The duties performed by lighthouses were not always rooted in solid, stationary, brick-built or iron towers. Similar duties were performed by lightships or light vessels. Each ship was equipped with a revolving light mounted at the top of a tall mast. The ships were placed in positions where the waters were too deep or otherwise unsuitable for lighthouse construction. Early lightships had no engines and were towed into position where they were anchored. Later, engines were installed.

The very first of the style that became synonymous with lightship design was positioned in the Thames Estuary in 1734 close to Havengore Creek in Essex to warn sailors of the dangers of the Nore Sandbank.

Lightship crews were in place to maintain the lights which were originally run up and down the mast for servicing, but later fixed with Fresnel lenses to enhance the light. It was a boring life for the men who manned the ships and many turned to hobbies such as toy making and fretwork to help pass the long hours spent on the ships away from home.

As lighthouse building became more advanced and automated buoys more practical, the Trinity House lightships were withdrawn from service, but at least three can still be found in Essex, where they have taken on new lives.

LV 18, a lightship permanently moored today at Harwich.

One, designated as Light Vessel 18, is moored at the end of the Ha'penny Pier in Harwich. In the 1960s, LV18 served in various spots around the coast, her final station being at Dowsing off the coast of East Anglia in the 1970s. The ship was retired from service in 1994, by which time she had become Trinity House's longest serving light vessel. Used for a while as the base for several pirate and restricted service radio stations, she took centre stage as the star of a film about a pirate radio station called *The Boat That Rocked*. Unfortunately, the scenes that contained LV18 were eventually cut from the finished film. She is now a permanent tourist attraction on Harwich Quay.

A second lightship can be found at King Edward Quay on the River Colne that flows through Colchester. This is the Colne Light, commissioned by Trinity House in 1953 and launched in 1954. The ship was damaged in 1960, but remained in service until she was decommissioned in 1988. These days she is used by the Colchester Sea Cadets charity and is also available for hire for private parties and business meetings.

A third lightship, built for Trinity House in 1954, now forms the centre point of the Fellowship Afloat charitable trust at Tollesbury close to the mouth of

The Colne Light is moored at King Edward Quay in Colchester.

The lightship at Tollesbury now forms the centre point for a charitable trust.

the River Blackwater, an area famous for its desolate marshes. Here the ship provides a place for arts, crafts and adventure activities. The vessel, called *Trinity*, was converted as a residential centre in 1990, keeping the exterior faithful to the original lightship design and with an interior in keeping with its original character.

The *Mayflower* Connection

When the Pilgrim Fathers left Britain for the New World on the *Mayflower* in 1620, it's well documented that they sailed from Plymouth. Consequently, Devon is the county that gets most associated with the voyage and the subsequent colonisation of America. The truth, however, is that the *Mayflower* had only a passing connection with Plymouth. Its origins are far more firmly rooted in Essex, where the ship was built and registered and where its captain lived and married.

Also, it wasn't even the first ship with Essex connections to take colonists to America. Thirteen years before the *Mayflower*'s more famous voyage, Seaman and Privateer Christopher Newport, who was born in Harwich, commanded three ships that, in 1607, took 144 passengers, many from Essex, to Chesapeake Bay where they established the settlement of Jamestown, named in honour of King James I. Newport's name and voyage are commemorated in Harwich on one of many wall plaques around the town, bringing information about people and events for which Harwich is famous.

It is of course its *Mayflower* connections that Harwich boasts about and celebrates most. A walk through the town reveals a road, restaurant, taxi company,

CHRISTOPHER NEWPORT
1561 - 1617
CHRISTOPHER NEWPORT WAS CHRISTENED IN ST. NICHOLAS' CHURCH, HARWICH, ESSEX, ON DECEMBER 29TH 1561. AFTER AN ADVENTUROUS SEAFARING CAREER IN THE WEST INDIES, THE VIRGINIA COMPANY APPOINTED HIM "SOLE COMMANDER" OF THE EXPEDITION THAT, IN 1607, ESTABLISHED JAMESTOWN, THE FIRST PERMANENT ENGLISH SETTLEMENT IN AMERICA. HE DIED IN 1617 ON A TRADING EXPEDITION TO JAVA.

ERECTED BY THE HARWICH SOCIETY

Christopher Newport's plaque in Harwich.

Mayflower Avenue in Harwich is named after the famous ship that took the Pilgrim Fathers to America.

school and medical centre all named after the ship, and at Dedham Vale Vineyard in nearby Colchester, a pale straw-coloured wine called Mayflower is brewed. There are also many murals on walls around Harwich that commemorate the voyage.

The *Mayflower*'s master was Captain Christopher Jones who lived in Harwich in a sixteenth-century house at No. 21 King's Head Street, close to the harbour. A plaque above the door states: 'The home of Captain Christopher Jones, Master of the Mayflower'. A short walk from the house is St Nicholas's Church. A church has stood on this site since 1177, but it was in the currently standing church that Captain Jones was twice married, once in 1593 and again, after his first wife died, in 1603.

It's no coincidence that both Captain Jones and the *Mayflower* came from this part of Essex. Much of England's shipbuilding in the seventeenth century was based in East Anglia, and the *Mayflower* was one among many ships built in the area. Captain Jones was born in 1570, the son of a mariner and shipowner. He rose to become a man of prominence in the local community and, in 1607, with three business partners, he purchased the *Mayflower*. Taking on the role of its master, he initially sailed it on trading missions up and down the Essex coast and to countries that included France, Norway, Spain and Germany before being hired to transport the Pilgrim Fathers on their historic journey in 1620. It was the ship's first Atlantic crossing.

By this time, Christopher Jones had moved to Rotherhithe, then a parish of Surrey, but now part of the South London Borough of Southwark. But that hasn't stopped Harwich celebrating his connections with the town in murals around the area. One depicts what Captain Jones might have looked like, along with his ship and house. Another shows the signing of the Mayflower Compact, a ceremony which took place during the voyage, and which many believe was a forerunner of the American Constitution.

The house in Harwich where *Mayflower* Master Christopher Jones lived.

THE HOME OF CAPTAIN CHRISTOPHER JONES MASTER OF THE MAYFLOWER

The plaque over the front door of Christopher Jones's house.

So with Essex in general, and Harwich in particular, being so closely connected to the *Mayflower*, why does Plymouth get all the accolades? The answer is purely by chance. The voyage officially began in Southampton on the south coast of England, with the *Mayflower* accompanied by a sister ship called the *Speedwell*. Unfortunately, the *Speedwell* soon began to leak, forcing the two ships to return to Dartmouth for repairs, before setting off again. Around 300 miles out to sea the *Speedwell* once more began to leak, so this time they returned to Plymouth, which, being west of both Dartmouth and Southampton, made a more convenient port of call. Here, the *Speedwell*'s cargo and many of its passengers were transferred to the already crowded *Mayflower*, which then, for the third time, set sail for the New World.

The other myth that brings Plymouth into the story is that the place where the Pilgrim Fathers landed was named Plymouth, after the place in Devon. In fact, the location had already been named New Plymouth (also known as Plimouth or Plimoth) by English soldier and explorer Captain John Smith and its name first appeared on maps in 1616, four years before the arrival of the *Mayflower*. Since the place from which they had sailed in England was coincidentally also called Plymouth, they elected to retain the name for their settlement. On the other hand, a trip of 46 miles from the American Plymouth, around the coast of Cape Cod Bay, reveals another ancient town whose name is more familiar to Essex people. It's called Harwich.

Murals around Harwich celebrate the town's connection with the *Mayflower*.

Ghostly Goings-on

Essex is an ancient county full of history and historic buildings, many of which are claimed to be the oldest of their type in the country. Whether every such claim is completely accurate or not, one thing remains true: where there are ancient buildings, reports of ghosts are never far behind. Essex abounds in such stories.

Borley Rectory

The Revd Henry Dawson Ellis Bull was the son of the Revd Edward Bull who built the Bull's Tower folly in Pentlow. When Edward Bull left Pentlow, he took up residence in Borley Place, a sixteenth-century house in the parish of Borley. It was here that Henry Bull grew up and, following his father's footsteps into the Church, built Borley Rectory to house his growing family and servants in 1863. The rectory was to become known as the most haunted house in England.

It was said that the house was built on the site of a thirteenth-century monastery, from where a monk had eloped with a nun from a nearby convent. There is no evidence of a monastery ever being built at Borley, but that hasn't stopped the story growing with claims that the monk was hanged, while the nun was bricked up alive in her convent. There followed numerous and regular tales of sightings around the house of the ghostly pair and the coach and horses in which they were said to have attempted their escape. Another story told of a nun who walked the rectory gardens in broad daylight, and who had been seen by Bull's daughters.

Over the coming years, as the rectory passed into the hands of other Bull family members, more stories of hauntings were told, but they peaked in the 1930s when more than 2,000 psychic occurrences were recorded in a five-year period. They

The ruins of Borley Rectory before it was demolished in 1944.

included mysterious footsteps inside the house, doorbells that seemed to ring of their own accord and many instances of poltergeist activity.

During this time, Harry Price, a renowned paranormal investigator of the era, moved in and claimed he had been in contact with the spirit of a previous owner who had died in the house. As new residents moved in, activity increased even more with stories of broken glasses, smashed windows and even the occupant of the house being flung forcibly from her bed. Messages were also said to have appeared on the walls. Paranormal activity decreased when those last residents left. Since then, many of the reports of paranormal activity have been analysed and exposed as fake or misinterpretations of the perfectly normal. But many of the alleged happenings have never been fully explained and the rectory has retained its 'most haunted house in England' reputation.

Borley Rectory unexpectedly burned down in 1939, probably as the result of an overturned oil lamp placed among a pile of books. The building was demolished in 1944.

Eastbury Manor House

Incongruously situated in the middle of a 1920s housing estate in Barking, the sixteenth-century Eastbury Manor House stands in its own surrounding gardens. It is a Grade I listed building built *c.* 1573 during the reign of Queen Elizabeth I and was once reckoned to be the place where the Gunpowder Plot's plan to assassinate King James I on his visit to Parliament was conceived in 1605. It is possible that there were links between the house and the plotters, but the story of it being the place where the plot originated has been largely discredited. Unsurprisingly, however, it has its fair share of alleged ghosts.

One story is that the house is haunted by the ghost of a young girl in period clothing, but who is only ever seen by women. Another tells the tale of a jilted bridegroom who hanged himself in one of the towers and is seen wandering around the house. Some say that the ghost of Clement Sysley, the man who built

Eastbury House is a Tudor manor house in the middle of a housing estate in Barking.

the house and who died there five years after its completion, can be seen floating around in Tudor costume. Groups of monks talking among themselves before vanishing into thin air are claimed to have been seen. Ghostly footsteps in the attic, strange entities flitting across the grounds, mysterious flashes of light and energy matter streaking across rooms have also been reported.

When it was built, Eastbury Manor House was located in an isolated and elevated position with views across marshland to the River Thames. Today, the house, all but lost in a maze of busy suburban roads, is managed by the London Borough of Barking and Dagenham Council on behalf of the National Trust. Despite it being a meeting place for many years of the Barking Photographic Society, no serious photographic evidence of the paranormal at the house has been forthcoming. Although who can say what might have been witnessed there before the days of photography?

The Oldest Pub in England

Halfway between Braintree and Chelmsford, in the village of Great Leighs, stands a pub that claims to be the oldest in England. Known today as The Castle, it was formerly called St Anne's Castle Inn. A plaque on its wall dates it to AD 1171. Its age is more apparent on the inside than the outside, which was renovated after a fire in the 1550s when its thatched roof was replaced by tiles. The remains of tunnels that lead from the cellars are thought to once have linked the pub to a local church and priory.

The Castle pub at Great Leighs, reputed to be the oldest pub in England.

The pub is said to be haunted by a man from the village who was hanged in 1875 for strangling his wife and son after discovering the boy was his brother's child. Other ghostly apparitions reported over the years include a small girl with blond curly hair, a little boy, a woman in a wedding dress and a customer who sits in the bar smoking his pipe.

The pub was also the centre of a story concerning a local witch called Anne Hughes who was burnt at the stake in the seventeenth century after allegedly bewitching her husband to death. When her remains were buried, a large, heavy stone was placed on her grave. All remained calm until, in the 1940s, bulldozers widening the road displaced the stone. After that, it is said, church bells rang at midnight, sheep and horses were found dead in fields and a large bolder appeared outside a village house without any known means of it getting there. At the same time, strange things began happening at the St Anne's Castle Inn. Strange noises were heard and items were moved around in rooms, then moved again after the rooms were tidied up. The occurrences only ceased when the witch's tombstone was returned to its original site. An eminent ghost hunter called in to assess the situation later concluded that while he thought some of the occurrences were the result of practical jokers, much was still left unexplained.

Hadleigh Castle

Situated to the south of the town of Hadleigh, this was once a royal castle, built during the reign of King Henry III in the 1230s for the 1st Earl of Kent and Chief Justice of England. In the fifteenth and sixteenth centuries it was part of the dowry of Elizabeth Woodville, wife of King Edward IV and three of King Henry VIII's wives: Catherine of Aragon, Anne of Cleves, and Catherine Parr. In

The remains of Hadleigh Castle, built in the thirteenth century.

later years, it was used as a source of stone for other buildings and was allowed to fall into ruin. Today two towers still stand, although one of them has largely disintegrated. None of which detracts from the fact that the castle remains are reckoned to be haunted.

One story tells of the meeting of a milkmaid called Sally with a haggard old lady who demanded that Sally revisit her at the castle at midnight. Scared to venture near the castle at that time of night, Sally failed to turn up, but was visited again by the ghostly old lady the next morning who, furious at Sally not returning as requested, hit her hard over the head and badly damaged her neck. It is reckoned that even today the old hag can still be heard cackling in the castle in the hours of night.

Coalhouse Fort

Coalhouse Fort that stands at Tilbury today was built in 1864 on the site of an old artillery fort and was used for coastal defence. It was still playing a part in warfare as late as the Second World War. In 1962 the fort was purchased by Thurrock Council and today is part of open parkland, linked by a footpath to nearby Tilbury Fort. It is Coalhouse Fort, however, that is known for its ghosts.

There is a washroom in the fort that is said to make visitors feel uncomfortable, and the longer they stay, the more disturbed they become. Chairs and other items of furniture are thrown across rooms by poltergeist activity, light bulbs explode and people claim to have seen dark figures walking towards them then vanishing. Some have even reported being physically touched or even grabbed by the

Coalhouse Fort in Tilbury is said to be haunted.

The Harwich Redoubt still exhibits rooms where soldiers lived in the nineteenth century.

visitations. Tunnels beneath the fort are particularly known for their hauntings, where visitors have reported hearing the heated voices of men in the middle of a poker game, as well as the laughter of small children.

Harwich Redoubt

The Redoubt is a fort just outside Harwich, built in the nineteenth century to protect the town from invasion. It still has rooms in which soldiers of the past lived, as well as cells where prisoners were detained. Naturally, it also has its ghost stories.

In one of the fort's rooms, it is said that a spirit resides and holds the hands of those who enter. Strange noises, apparitions and cold spots within rooms have also been reported. As recently as 1972, a soldier at the fort was decapitated by a cable that broke under the strain of lifting a huge and heavy cannon. Naturally, his headless body has been seen walking around the grounds with his decapitated head under its arm.

Layer Marney Tower

The tallest gatehouse in Britain is said to be haunted by Lord Henry Marney, the man who died before work on his grand country residence was completed, as he laments the fact the tower was not built in the way he had envisaged it. Sometimes he is seen on horseback, in full armour, setting off for battle.

Red Lion Hotel

Since Colchester is the oldest recorded town in Britain, it stands to reason that one of its oldest hotels is reputed to be haunted. The Red Lion is actually a coaching inn built in 1465 and still retains its original Tudor features, both inside and outside.

For many years, visitors to the hotel have reported seeing the ghost of a woman roaming the hotel corridors and appearing particularly in three rooms. The ghost is said to be that of Alice Miller, a chambermaid at the hotel who, in 1638, was thrown from one of the windows by a wealthy businessman who had had an affair with her, but whose feelings changed when he discovered she was pregnant.

The Red Lion Hotel in Colchester, where the ghost of a woman is reputed to have been seen.

Her murder became one of Colchester's most infamous crimes. In the mid-1800s, the hotel's owner became so annoyed by guests claiming to have seen the ghost that he bricked up the door to what had been Alice's room. It made no difference and there are those who say she still appears today, sometimes wandering around the kitchen, or walking through the bricked-up wall to her old room.

The hotel is also reputed to be haunted by the ghost of a hooded monk who died in a fire there in the 1800s, trying to save some children. A small boy is also sometimes seen, mostly by children, and some say he even appears in guests' photographs.

Mersea's Ghostly Centurion

At the time when the Romans occupied Britain with their capital at Camulodunum, the town known today as Colchester, there was a garrison for soldiers at nearby Mersea Island, which lies at the end of a causeway known as The Strood. It's here that on moonlit October nights, residents and visitors have reported seeing the ghost of a Roman centurion as he patrols the road between the mainland and the island. There are many different variations on the way the centurion is seen or heard.

One version states that he can be seen only from the waist up, because he is marching on the original road which, in Roman times, was a few feet below the causeway as it is today. There have been other reports of drivers who suddenly see him in their headlights, vanishing as they pass by. It seems the centurion is sometimes heard but not seen, as stories of ghostly footsteps following walkers across The Strood have been reported. Marching soldiers, the sound of cartwheels on stone and heavy fighting with the clash of swords have also been described, even at times of high tide when the sea covers The Strood.

Other Lesser-known Essex Ghosts

In Basildon, legend has it that running anti-clockwise around Holy Cross Church conjures up the apparition of a red-robed monk who drifts across the road and through the wall of the church.

Above left: The Strood that connects Mersea Island to the mainland, where a ghostly Roman centurion has sometimes been seen.

Above right: The Cage at St Osyth, now refurbished, but once one of the many buildings in the area said to be haunted.

Similarly, running around All Saints' Church in Chelmsford at midnight is reckoned to cause the ghost of an angry nun to appear and chase after you.

In Brentwood there is a duck pond that used to be bigger than it is today. One night, some say, a farmer and his horse fell into it. Others claim that it was only a horse and wagon that went into the water. Either way, the ghostly whinny of a horse might be heard in the vicinity at night.

At Canvey Island, there is another pond that is reputed to be haunted by the ghost of a man, or maybe a woman, or even a horse and cart. One or all of them are said to have lost their way in the dark and sunk in the mud around the lake. Others claim that they were trying to cross the frozen lake when the ice cracked and they fell through. In the 1980s the lake was dredged and part of a horse's skull was found, along with cartwheels.

One more pond in the grounds of a priory at Prittlewell is said to be haunted by the ghost of a bride who downed there. A ghostly monk has also been known to make an alleged appearance.

The ghost of a hooded man and a monk who was executed are regular visitors to Beeleigh Abbey in Maldon, where poltergeist activity has also been recorded.

The Cage is a building at St Osyth that was once used as a prison. The ghosts of people who were imprisoned and executed there as far back as 1582 are still seen by some. Poltergeist activity is also occasionally apparent.

Theatres are always known for their ghosts, and the Palace Theater in Southend-on-Sea is no exception. Members of the audience say they have felt the presence and touch of a ghostly hand from someone sitting in an empty seat beside them. Actors at the theatre have reported strange smells of tobacco backstage when no one has been smoking. The sound of a piano in the orchestra pit has also been reported.

St Osyth was named after a seventh-century East Anglian queen who was executed close to a local priory. The story goes that, following her execution, she bent down, picked up her severed head and walked with it to the priory. Her ghost is said to repeat the walk on certain nights each October.

St Peter-on-the-Wall is a church in Bradwell dating back to *c.* AD 650. Today, according to some, it is home to ghostly figures that walk around the interior, from where an eerie light shines in the night.

These are just some of the very many ghost stories that are told around Essex. Often the stories get debunked by experts in the field, or else it is proven that they are no more than legends that have grown up and become exaggerated over the years. But still there are stories that remain unexplained and, to those who claim to have witnessed them, ghosts, poltergeists and other unworldly apparitions are very much alive and well in this ancient county.

St Osyth Priory, named after an East Anglian queen who was beheaded nearby.

Religious Curiosities

Essex has a great many historic churches. Clearly, a whole book could be written on the subject, of which there is far more to say than can be encompassed in these few pages. So, here's a more concise look at just four unusual churches, one historically important abbey and the second smallest cathedral in Britain.

St Andrew's Church, Greenstead

Close to the town of Chipping Ongar, the small village of Greenstead boasts the oldest wooden church in the world, at least in part. It is also thought that the earliest fragments of the church represent the oldest wooden building in Europe still standing.

The fifty-one timber planks that make up the oldest part of the church date back to 1060. Excavation in the 1960s uncovered even earlier timber structures that date back to the sixth and seventh centuries, a time when Saint Cedd was beginning his work on converting the Saxons to Christianity.

In 1013, the body of Saint Edmund, the King of East Anglia, rested in the church on its way to Bury St Edmunds in Suffolk. The oldest grave in the churchyard is thought to be that of a bowman from the twelfth-century crusades.

In the wooden wall of the side of the church, on the farthest side from its entrance, there is a small aperture built into the woodwork. It's possible that this was no more than a tiny window to enable those inside to see who was approaching the church. But a far more interesting theory is that it was a lepers' squint, from which local people suffering from leprosy and banned from entering the church could still receive a blessing from the priest.

St Andrew's Church in Greenstead dates back to 1060.

The leper's squint in the wall of St Andrew's Church.

The mysterious Mistley Towers.

The Parish Church of Mistley

In the north Essex village of Mistley overlooking the River Stour, two magnificent and classically ornate towers stand incongruously each side of the entrance to a small cemetery. Built in the neoclassical style, they take the form of slender pavilions, decorated with Ionic columns and cornices, each topped by a cupola. Today, they seem to serve no real purpose, but in the 1770s, they stood at either end of an unusual parish church.

This was a time when civil servant and politician Richard Rigby of Mistley Hall was Chief Secretary of Ireland and Paymaster General of the Forces. Mistley at this time was a trading port, but Rigby decided to take the area more upmarket, calling in architect Robert Adam to help turn Mistley into a fashionable spa. Although the plan didn't come to fruition, Adam's services were retained to build a new parish church with a brief for it to be grand and easily seen from the windows of Rigby's mansion.

When it was built, it resembled a small cathedral more than a parish church. In the eighteenth century, most churches followed the traditional design of a rectangular building with a tower on the western end. But Adam's ideas were far from traditional. Out went convention and in came an architectural design featuring towers at both eastern and western ends of the building. The church that lay between the towers was small by comparison, a single storey with a pitched roof and ornamental entrance porches on the north and south sides. Today, a sign at the entrance to the cemetery shows how it looked.

The parish church of Mistley stood for nearly 100 years, but in 1870, it was replaced by a more fashionable Gothic Revival church built nearby. The main body of the old church was demolished, but the towers were allowed to remain intact. Two local families bought them with the intention of using them as mausoleums. It never happened, and the towers fell onto disrepair. They were restored to their former glory in the 1950s.

How the towers were once part of a church.

All Saints' at Wrabness, a church without a tower.

All Saints', Wrabness

A few miles east of Mistley, in the village of Wrabness, another church appears, at first sight, to be of a far more conventional design, apart from one detail: it has no tower. All Saints' dates back to the twelfth century and, originally, had a tower that housed five bells. In the seventeenth century the roof of the chancel and the tower both collapsed. The roof was rebuilt, but the tower wasn't. Instead, two of the bells were placed in wooden structures in the courtyard. It was intended to be a temporary solution but 300 years later, they are still there, and can be seen in the churchyard.

St Mary the Virgin, Tilty

In the village of Tilty there is an unusual-looking church that appears to be two churches from different eras joined together. The oldest part of the building was originally a chapel that stood at the gates of Tilty Abbey, built in the twelfth

The bells of All Saints', contained in a wooden cage in the graveyard.

St Mary the Virgin, looking like two churches joined together.

century. It was ordained that the church could be used by women, children and others not allowed into the abbey grounds, which were the sole domain of the monks who resided in the abbey.

Abbey and church existed together for around 400 years until the abbey was dissolved in 1536, when parts were turned into private dwellings, while other parts were robbed for building materials. Very soon little remained, apart from the small church that stood at the abbey gates, to be used as the local church for the people of Tilty.

In the eighteenth century, a porch and bell turret, built in a style commensurate with that age, rather than in the medieval style of the original church, were added. The two parts of the same church still stand joined together today. All that remains of the abbey are a couple chunks of stone wall in a field beyond the church.

Chelmsford Cathedral

Situated within a pedestrianised shopping area, Chelmsford Cathedral is officially known as the Cathedral Church of St Mary, St Peter and St Cedd. It was originally built as a parish church in the thirteenth century and completely rebuilt 200 years later. In 1800, repairs undermined a pillar that caused the nave to collapse. No one was injured and a new rhyme, involving the nearby village of Writtle, entered popular folklore:

Chelmsford Church and Writtle steeple
Fell down one day but killed no people.

The exterior of the cathedral is particularly striking, with its fifteenth-century tower topped by a lantern that dates to 1749. The two-storey south porch also dates from the fifteenth century and features architectural flushwork, a treatment that uses flints to form decorative patterns.

The Cathedral Church of St Mary, St Peter and St Cedd, otherwise known as Chelmsford Cathedral.

The church was raised to cathedral status in 1914, even though Chelmsford didn't attain city status until 2012 to mark the Diamond Jubilee of Queen Elizabeth II, making it England's youngest city. At 11,270 square feet, Chelmsford Cathedral is the second smallest cathedral in England, being only slightly larger than the 10,950 square feet of Derby Cathedral.

Barking Abbey

On the edge of Barking, where the town meets the River Roding, there stands a stone tower. Today it forms the entrance to St Margaret's Church, but once it marked an entrance to one of the most important nunneries in the country.

Barking Abbey was founded in AD 666, destroyed by the Vikings in AD 871 and subsequently rebuilt when the English regained control of the area. It was built as a Benedictine nunnery and, under the patronage of King Edgar, received estates and revenue that helped it become rich and powerful. It remained so for another half century or more until King Henry VIII began the Dissolution of the Monasteries in 1536. Demolition began in 1540, with its stonework and lead from the roof pillaged for use in various royal residences.

Today only two buildings and the outlines of a few footings remain. St Margaret of Antioch Church, usually referred to more simply as St Margaret's, which once stood within the grounds of the abbey, is still in full-time use as

Curfew Tower at Barking, which once stood at the entrance to Barking Abbey.

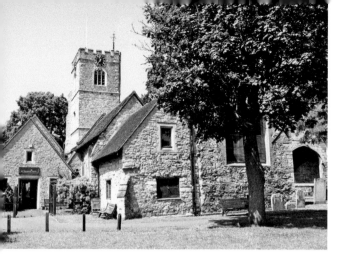

Left: St Margaret's Church originally stood in the grounds of Barking Abbey.

Below: Part of the ruins of Barking Abbey.

Baking's parish church. It's where the explorer Captain James Cook was married on 21 December 1762.

The stone tower that once marked an entrance to the abbey is variously known as the Bell Tower or Curfew Tower. It takes its name from the times when an unusual local custom decreed people of the town should extinguish and relight all fires and candles at certain hours of the day. The bell in the tower tolled as a reminder that it was time to start the ritual.

In the days when Barking Abbey thrived as a famous nunnery, it incorporated an asylum for the insane. Some claim that this was the origins of the expression 'barking mad', although others will point out that the expression probably didn't come into use until the twentieth century – more than 350 years after the abbey and its asylum were demolished.

Underground Essex

There is something about an underground tunnel that creates a sense of intrigue, maybe because the word 'tunnel' is so often associated with the word 'secret'. Essex is riddled with secret tunnels, some of which can still be seen, many of which have vanished in the mists of time. Then there are those that existed only as rumours, legends handed down from generation to generation about covert passages between ancient buildings, often with stories of ghosts and, near the coast, tales of smugglers. Whether many of the tunnels of Essex still exist, once existed or never existed at all, the stories about them each have one thing in common: a sense of secretive mystery.

Kelvedon Hatch Secret Nuclear Bunker

At Kelvedon Hall Lane, in Kelvedon Hatch near Brentwood, there stands a bungalow that looks like an innocent farm cottage. It was built this way to disguise the fact that it was actually the entrance to a tunnel that led to a secret underground bunker.

After the end of the Second World War in 1945, and in the shadow of the atom bombs dropped on Hiroshima and Nagasaki, a Cold War developed that led to a real fear of nuclear attack from Soviet Russia. It was in this climate that the secret nuclear bunker was built in 1952. Its purpose was to house the British government, including the prime minister, with the hundreds of people needed to run the country and maintain law and order in the wake of a nuclear attack on Britain. Once in the bunker, blast doors would be closed and there would be enough provisions and facilities on hand to sustain 600 military, civilian and governmental people below ground for three months.

The entrance to the secret bunker at Kelvedon Hatch.

An underground corridor in the bunker.

The bunker still exists. It is encased in 10-foot-thick concrete walls and built on three floors, containing areas that include a plotting room, communications rooms, dormitories, washrooms, a hospital, operating theatre, a canteen and mortuary. It was designed to be totally self-sufficient, with supplies of water, generators for electricity, air purifiers for filtering outside air from radioactive contamination before feeding it into the bunker and a cooling plant to keep the entire place at a comfortable temperature.

In the past the bunker has been used as an RAF Rotor radar station, the regional government headquarters for which it is most famous and a civil defence centre. Today it is privately owned and run as a tourist attraction. The roads surrounding it are full of road signs pointing the way to the 'Secret Nuclear Bunker', which clearly isn't quite so secret anymore.

Great Baddow's Secret Tunnels

Although it has never been proven, there are stories in Great Baddow about a network of tunnels beneath the seventeenth-century White Horse pub. They are said to have once run along beneath the buildings that adjoin the pub and that there is also a tunnel from here to nearby St Mary's Church.

The story goes that a monk was once trapped and died in these tunnels when the exit was bricked in and that his ghost has haunted the church ever since. His ghostly figure has been seen moving along the church's aisles and between the pews and always leaves by the west door. The current church tower was built at this spot during the fourteenth century after the west wall was removed, and it is thought that the place where the monk vanishes was once the church's main exit.

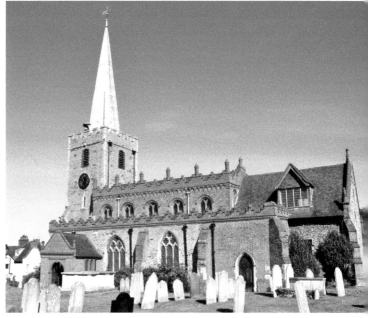

Above: The White Horse at Great Baddow.

Below right: St Mary's Church, Great Baddow.

Hadleigh Castle's Tunnels

Known for its stories of ghosts and hauntings, Hadleigh Castle is also the focal point of what is thought to have been a maze of tunnels spreading out across the Essex countryside.

One such tunnel led from the castle to the nearby riverbed, which indicates it might once have been used by smugglers coming up the river and needing a way to secretly access a place to stash their ill-gotten gains in the castle.

Another tunnel is reputed to have run from the castle to the cellar of Castle House, which was part of a farm built in 1706, but demolished in 1974. Rochford Hall, around 4 miles away, might once have had its own tunnel that linked back to the castle. On Canvey Island, a house on Denham Road and a farm reputed to have once been a chapel were also the starting or ending point for underground passages back to Hadleigh Castle.

Harlow's Tunnels

The new town that is generally thought of when mention is made of Harlow was built after the Second World War to help ease overcrowding in London. Long before this modern conurbation sprung into existence, however, the original town of Harlow, now more popularly known as Old Harlow, had been standing at this location. Now an extension of the eastern part of the new town, the original town dates back to a time before the first written records of the Domesday Book, the manuscript that set out to record a survey of England and much of Wales at the instigation of William the Conqueror in 1086.

St Mary's Church, Old Harlow.

The Queen's Head at Old Harlow, said to be linked by a tunnel to the nearby church.

Beneath this ancient town there lies what is believed to be a labyrinth of underground passages. One links St Mary's Church to the Queen's Head Inn and the nearby Stafford Alms Houses, both built in the seventeenth century. In around 1630, a priest lived in the latter building, where he built a chapel in the cellar. Conversion work carried out as late as 1970 discovered evidence of a tunnel leading from here to a still-standing seventeenth-century hotel and two manor houses.

The Mersea Island Barrow

In East Mersea Road, soon after crossing from the mainland onto Mersea Island, there is an unnatural-looking mound of grass with trees growing on it. This is variously known as Mersea Mound, Mersea Mount and Grim's Hoe. In fact, it's a Roman burial barrow. Barrows date back way past Roman times and are known to have existed in the middle Neolithic period of around 3500–2700 BC. Strictly speaking, they are not under the ground, but built above it before being covered with a mound of stone and soil.

The Mersea Island barrow was most likely a Roman burial barrow dating to AD 100–120. It was excavated in 1912, when an entrance passage was built, leading to the centre of the mound in which was found a Roman-built burial chamber. In the chamber there was a lead box containing an urn of green glass and the cremated remains of a body. Much later, in 2013, the contents of the urn were analysed by experts who revealed that they were the bones of a man between

Above: The Mersea barrow.

Left: The entrance to the barrow.

Inside the Mersea barrow.

the ages of thirty-five and forty-five. He might have had British ancestors, but it was clear that he lived as a Roman and was buried in a high-status tomb.

Mersea contains the remains of several Roman villas, and it's probable that the man was cremated on a funeral pyre near where the barrow was constructed close to his home. The bones were covered in a mysterious sticky substance that was later identified as frankincense. Although best known as a gift from one of the Three Wise Men in the traditional story of the nativity, frankincense was actually more often used in different cultures for medical and religious purposes.

Smugglers' Tunnels

Essex is a coastal county and one that is full of creeks and inlets that were a godsend to smugglers of old. Wherever there was a place along the coast where smugglers could land in secret, stories would grow up of tunnels along which they could carry their booty to a place where it might be safely stored, or for them to flee along when they needed to escape the law. The tunnels nearly always led from the coast to either a church or an inn. Here are some of the tunnels known or merely rumoured to have existed.

In Fobbing there was a tunnel from the Creek to St Michael's Church. There was a story that told of the Devil chasing smugglers down the tunnel who was after their souls. The smugglers slammed a door at the end of the tunnel on him and it was said that, for many years, it bore the imprint of the Devil's claws.

Southend-on-Sea was once the centre of a great deal of smuggling activity – and where there were smugglers, there were bound to be stories of tunnels. One was said to lead from the coast to an eighteenth-century house, which today is a preparatory school. The building is said to be haunted by a ghost carrying a lantern.

At South Benfleet, Jarvis Hall beside Thundersley Park Road, smugglers supposedly used a tunnel that linked the hall to St Mary the Virgin Church, a mile away. Another tunnel is said to have run from the church to a fifteenth-century pub in Benfleet High Street.

More smugglers are connected with a tunnel to a building in Southend-on-Sea, now used as a civic venue, but once a sixteenth-century house called Porters. From here to the seafront, smugglers were reputed to have built a tunnel.

St Nicholas' Church, Harwich.

Harwich, where the River Stour meets the North Sea in North Essex, is well known for stories of smugglers who built a tunnel from the basement of a former bakery in King's Quay Street to St Nicholas's Church, a few streets inland.

Other Essex Tunnel Legends

At the Fox and Fiddler pub in St John's Street, Colchester, a labyrinth of cellars and tunnels were said to lead all over the town.

At Thorrington, a country house contained a tunnel from a reputed haunted room to nearby St Osyth's Priory.

At Maldon, a tunnel once linked All Saints' Church in the town to Beeleigh Abbey, whose remains still exist.

While married to Catherine of Aragon, King Henry VIII and Anne Boleyn are said to have met in secret in a tunnel that was part of a network running under Rochford Hall in Rochford.

Colchester Castle is said to be connected by a tunnel to the twelfth-century Coggeshall Abbey.

Catholics seeking to escape persecution in Tudor times are reckoned to have fled along a tunnel that ran from a mansion house in the village of Wimbish to Hortham Hall in Thaxted.

At Stapleford Abbots, on the site of a fourteenth-century manor house there is still the bricked-up entrance to two tunnels that led to two nearby farms.

On the Dengie peninsular, in the small village of Steeple, a tunnel is rumoured to link the seventeenth-century Star Inn with St Laurence's Church, which was built in 1884 on the site of an older medieval structure that was destroyed by fire.

Dominating the centre of the village of St Osyth, the remains of an ancient priory mark the start of a tunnel that terminates in the cellar of a building called the Old House, dating back to 1300 and once known as Priory Cottages.

At Horndon on the Hill, legend has it that a subterranean passage connects the church of St Peter and St Paul with the fifteenth-century Bell Inn, standing in the village's nearby High Road.

If legends and stories, many of which are definitely apocryphal, are to be believed, Essex was once undermined by tunnels and passageways. Mostly the stories date back hundreds of years, so it is not surprising that so little evidence survives of tunnels that long ago collapsed or were filled in. With the exception of places like the Kelvedon Hatch Secret Nuclear Bunker that, in relative terms, was built fairly recently, there is little to see today of what might – or might not – have been entrances and exits to the tunnels of Essex. All that remains are a great many ancient buildings – many of them churches and antiquated inns – that might once have been linked by a veritable labyrinth of secret tunnels.

Beside the Seaside

Seaside resorts and pleasure piers have gone side by side since the early 1800s when the first English piers were built. Originally, they were used as landing stages for tourists taking boat trips, but then in Victorian times more and more people flocked to the coast to take the sea air. As the resorts prospered, so the piers took on new lives as places of entertainment. The wood of the original structures was replaced by decorative ironwork and many piers featured ornate pavilions which often appeared top heavy for the delicate structures that supported them. Essex, with its history as a popular destination for holidaymakers in times past, boasts four historic piers, at Southend, Clacton, Walton-on-the-Naze and Harwich.

Southend Pier

At 1.34 miles, Southend Pier is the longest pleasure pier in the world, but it wasn't always that way. A first wooden jetty was erected at the spot as far back as 1802, though its earliest plans as a wooden pier were proposed in 1828. Construction began but in 1829 a gale washed what had so far been built out to sea. Work immediately began again and the pier opened in 1830 with a length of 600 feet. It was extended to 1.25 miles in 1846, making it even then the longest pleasure pier

Southend Pier in 1909.

in the world. In 1885 a replacement iron pier was planned and the first third of its length opened to the public in 1889, soon to be extended with a second section. As more visitors came to Southend, the pier was extended again in 1898. An upper deck was added in 1908 and, in 1929, it was extended to its present length.

One reason why the pier is so long is because at this point on the Essex coast, where the Thames Estuary meets the North Sea, the tide has always retreated so far that boats needed to dock much further from the shore than might be the case in other resorts.

In 1890, an electric tramway was installed, consisting of a single carriage, increased to two carriages when the pier was extended and later transformed again with two trains supporting seven carriages each. In 1949 four new trains were installed with designs similar to those used on the London Underground. The tramway fell into disrepair and the trains stopped running in 1978, but in 1984, repairs were made and new tracks were laid. Today, two diesel-hydraulic trains run to the end of the pier and back on a single track with a passing loop.

Many times in its history, the pier has been damaged by boats that collided with it. In 1895 a collision with a Thames Lighter Barge sliced the pier in two. In 1898, a 100-foot section was damaged by another collision. Further damage was caused by collisions with passing ships in 1907, 1908, 1933 and as late as 1986, when the pier was again sliced in two by a colliding ship. During the Second World War, it was attacked several times by German bombers.

Southend Pier officially entered the *Guinness Book of Records* as the longest pleasure pier in the world in 2012.

Southend Pier
today.

Clacton Pier

Clacton Pier's history began in 1866 when an engineer from the town named Peter Bruff was given permission by the government to build a railway line into Clacton, with a pier to be used for the landing of goods, with a set scale of charges. They included sixpence (2½p) for a barrel of gunpowder, one penny (around ½p) per cubic foot for musical instruments, 2s 6d (12½p) for turtles and £1 for a corpse. The pier was completed and open to the public in 1871.

Within a decade, the pier's purpose began to change from business use to a place for tourists to enjoy the use of dining rooms, as well as hot and cold sea baths. At the same time, its length was increased to 1,180 feet. This made it easy for paddle steamers to land and depart at any time of the day, rather than having to wait for high tides. Visitors, then, came to the pier by land at one end and by boat at the other. In 1893 the Pier Pavilion was built for entertainment purposes and became one of only two theatres in the town.

During the First World War, between 1914 and 1918, visitors dwindled and the pier went bankrupt, to be saved by businessman Ernest Kingsman. Over the following years, Kingsman transformed the derelict pier into a major entertainment complex with two theatres, a large amusement hall and a casino. Later he widened the entrance and added more attractions that included a full-size Olympic standard swimming pool.

Clacton Pier in 1911.

Steel Stella on fire.

The pier's major attraction, for which it and the town of Clacton became famous, was a huge roller coaster, referred to by some as a switch-back. Its real name was Steel Stella, despite much of it being made of wood.

By the end of the 1930s as many as 40,000 people a day visited, but the outbreak of the Second World War in 1939 spelt doom for the pier. First it was badly damaged by a floating mine, then the Ministry of War declared that part of it should be destroyed to prevent the possibility of it being used as a landing stage in times of a possible German invasion. Consequently, a huge hole was blown in the middle of the pier, destroying the casino and one of the theatres. Only pleas from Ernest Kingsman prevented the government from also destroying Steel Stella.

Kingsman died during the war, but when hostilities ended in 1945, his son Barney took over, repaired the damage and added new attractions, before selling the pier in 1971.

In 1973, Steel Stella caught fire and was completely destroyed, very nearly taking the rest of the pier with it. When the roller coaster was dismantled, its remains were placed at the entrance to the pier for anyone to take away and use as firewood. Steel Stella's final legacy proved to be useful in the coming winter that was known for powerful gales and threats of power cuts.

The pier's popularity declined, but after its acquisition by a series of new owners and entrepreneurs who invested serious money in the enterprise, it still stands today, maybe not as popular as it was in its glory days, but still a major attraction of the town and living up to a nickname that it first acquired back in the 1930s, and which is now displayed in lights at the entrance: No. 1 North Sea.

Clacton Pier today.

Walton-on-the-Naze Pier

The first pier built at Walton-on-the-Naze was 330 feet long, made of wood and cost £1,000 to construct. It was opened in 1830. With seats along its length, it was used as a landing stage for steam packets travelling from London and Ipswich that docked at its end during high tides. In 1880, the pier was washed away by heavy seas, but not before a second pier had been built a little way along the shoreline.

The second pier opened in 1871 at 530 feet long, then was later rebuilt in 1898 to a length of 2,600 feet, which incorporated an electric tramway that ran along its length. That lasted until 1935, at which point it was replaced by an electric, battery-driven vehicle with rubber tyres that ran between two beams. Both the pier and the electric car were damaged by fire in 1942 during the Second World War, but the pier reopened after the war in 1948, this time with a diesel locomotive running along its length. That stopped operating in the 1970s.

In 1978, a lifeboat station which had been situated at the end of the pier since 1900 was cut off from the land by a huge storm that left a wide gap between the station and the rest of the pier.

The pier was put up for sale in 2011, but its high cost – in the millions – failed to attract a buyer. It was eventually bought in 2016 by a businessman with plans to return the pier to its glory days. Today the pier still pulls in tourists with attractions that include fairground rides, a ten-pin bowling alley and facilities for fishermen. It is the third longest pier in the UK.

The Harwich Ha'penny Pier

At the town quay in Harwich, the Ha'penny Pier was built in 1853. It was originally called the Corporation Pier, but the name was changed in reference to the days when admission was charged at half a penny, or ha'penny (less than a quarter of today's decimal 1p). Unusually the pier is L-shaped, enclosing a body of water known as The Pound, in which one of the UK's last surviving lightships is moored.

In Victorian times, the pier marked the departure point for cross-Channel ships, as well as local paddle steamers. It remained so up until the outbreak of the First World War in 1914 when it was used by the Royal Navy. Originally the pier was twice its present length, but fire destroyed part of it in 1927.

Walton Pier in the early 1900s.

Walton Pier today.

At the entrance to the pier, an ornate nineteenth-century toll booth still survives from the days when visitors paid their ha'pennies to promenade along its length or join a paddle steamer at its end. Today, the small building is home to the local historical society.

Renovated in 2017, the Harwich Ha'penny Pier is one of the UK's last surviving wooden, working piers.

Ha'penny Pier in Harwich in 1900.

The old tollbooth of the Ha'penny
Pier today.

Myths and Legends

Essex is a county full of legends. They range from stones and even whole churches which were said to move in the night, to tales of both Christian miracles and the Devil's handiwork. Some are based on real facts; others are no more than stories that became rumours that grew into legends destined to be exaggerated more and more over the years. Some tell the same story from different viewpoints; others give different interpretations of similar stories. The real fact is that the whole of this book could be filled with them, but here are just a few of the more intriguing myths that have come from this sometimes most mysterious of counties.

St George and the Dragon

According to legend, St George slew a dragon that had been terrorising a village, demanding the sacrifice of beautiful maidens. When the only maiden left in the village was the king's daughter, it was up to St George to kill the dragon, save the princess and ride into the history books. All of which was supposed to have happened in Libya during the thirteenth century. Or it might have been in Cappadocia, a Roman province of what is today central-eastern Turkey, during the eleventh century. It shows how legends develop, because although St George was made England's Patron Saint in 1350, he actually died a century before in AD 303 and never set foot in England.

Despite all of which, there is a myth that St George actually slew the dragon, not in Libya or Cappadocia, but in the Essex village of Wormingford during the thirteenth century. The story goes that a fire-breathing dragon came out of the River Stour and began devouring members of the local population. Sacrificial virgins were rumoured to be a way of pacifying the beast, but when the village ran out of virgins, a local knight, Sir George of Layer de la Haye, was called in to slay the beast. Some say he slew the dragon with his lance. Others claim he cut down a tree that fell on the beast and killed it. Either way, the village of Wormingford is named after the incident, 'worm' being an early word for dragon.

The story could have some basis in fact. It's possible that King Richard I brought a crocodile back to England from his time in the Crusades. It was kept in a cage in the Tower of London, but escaped into the River Thames. From there it found its way down the river to Essex and into the River Stour. When it first made an appearance in Sudbury, the terrorised locals tried to fight it off with bows and arrows, which bounced off its tough skin and scaly back. Some while later, the crocodile emerged again at Wormingford. Reports of its fiery breath were obviously exaggerated.

Wormingford town sign celebrates
St George and the dragon.

Today the dragon-slaying myth is celebrated by a weathervane on
Wormingford's town sign that depicts a knight on horseback fighting a dragon, a
stained-glass window in a local church, which also depicts a knight on horseback
involved in a fight with a dragon and a wall painting in the church of St Mary the
Virgin at nearby Wissingham that illustrates a fire-eating dragon.

Shakespeare in Essex

There is no evidence that William Shakespeare ever lived in Essex. But there have always been theories to suggest that some other playwrights might have had a lesser or greater hand in writing some of the plays attributed to the bard. Among those put forward as likely authors of Shakespeare's work are playwright Christopher Marlowe and writer, scientist and essayist Sir Francis Bacon. For some, however, the most likely candidate is Edward de Vere, poet, 7th Earl of Oxford and Lord Great Chamberlain of England. He lived at Hedingham Castle in the Essex village of Hedingham.

In 1918, English writer and teacher J. Thomas Looney originated the Oxfordian Theory which put forward the suggestion that de Vere was the true author of Shakespeare's plays. His reasoning involved the way events and characters in the plays might correspond to the life of the alleged author. After studying the biographies of a number of Elizabethan aristocrats, he became convinced that the life of de Vere, his career and many of his personal experiences corresponded

Heddingham Castle, the home of Edward de Vere.

strongly with the plots of a significant number of Shakespeare's plays. He set out his theories at length in a book called *Shakespeare Identified*, published in 1920.

In fact, despite Looney's interesting theories, there is little real evidence to suggest that de Vere did write any of the plays, although some believe there are references in the plays to the earl's life and that there are a series of codes in the writing that implicate him as the author.

Today Hedingham Castle is still standing and is the venue for weddings and events that include jousting, classic car shows and theatrical performances, including the plays of Shakespeare.

Old King Cole

Old King Cole was a merry old soul,
And a merry old soul was he.
He called for his pipe, and he called for his bowl,
And he called for his fiddlers three.

In the days when children were brought up on the old traditional nursery rhymes, this one was well known. What is less known is the identity of King Cole, when he lived and where he came from. The rhyme is reckoned to date back to the very early 1700s. If Essex legend is to be believed, King Cole – variously also named Coel and Coyle – came from, and gave his name to, what is now Colchester.

One line of thought is that the name of Colchester was derived from a third-century fortification named Coel's Castle, owned by a king whose name has come down in history as King Cole. Although this claim might not lie in fact, it is likely that this probably fictious king's name was based on Cunobelinus, who ruled much of southern Britain in the early part of the first century.

Further links between the nursery rhyme king and the town of Colchester can be found in Balkerne Castle, which now lies in ruins but which, until the nineteenth century, was known as Colkyng's Castle. Colchester Castle was built on the site of an old Roman temple called the Palace of Coel, at a time when a public well nearby was known as King Coyle's Pump. The pump is still in existence under the pavement at the junction of High Street, Head Street and North Hill. Within Colchester Castle, the great hall was once known as King Coel's Hall.

Outside the town of Colchester there lies a huge bowl-shaped depression in the land. Though once thought to have been a Roman amphitheatre, it is more likely to have been a gravel pit or quarry dating back to Roman times. The area is known as King Coel's Kitchen. Although partially filled, the depression can still be seen today to the west of King Coel Road.

The Oldest Tree in Essex

Close to the village pond in Fingringhoe there stands a massive oak tree whose girth spans more than 22 feet. It is said to be around 600 years old. The story goes that a smuggler or highwayman or pirate (local legends suggest all of these) was hanged outside the nearby churchyard and buried on this spot. But before he was buried, an acorn was placed in his mouth, from which grew this mighty oak, now reckoned to be the oldest tree in the county. It has become known as the Highwayman's Tree or the Fingringhoe Oak.

The St Osyth Miracle

If legend is to be believed, St Osyth (or Osgyth), after whom the town in Essex is named, didn't exactly lead a charmed life. As a child, during the first century AD, she fell into a river and drowned, but after three days she was resurrected from the dead with help of a saint called St Modwen, whom she had been on the way to visit when the accident happened. Modwen found her lifeless body on the banks of the river and prayed for her to rise from the dead, which she did.

At an early age Osyth took a vow of lifelong chastity and, when she was forced to marry Sighere, King of the East Saxons, the marriage was never consummated.

Fingringhoe oak tree, reckoned to be the oldest in Essex.

Nevertheless, the king gave her a village called Cise or Chich, which later became St Osyth. Here she established a nunnery where she reigned as the Abbess.

Then, in AD 630, Danes landed on the Essex coast. Arriving at the nunnery, the marauders destroyed the building and cut off the Abbess's head. At which point, she should have died for the second time. Instead, she picked up her own head and made her way to the nearest church, where she knocked on the door before falling to ground and finally dying. It became known as the St Osyth Miracle.

At the place where she had been beheaded, a well opened up and its waters became a fountain. Thereafter, St Osyth's Well became a place of pilgrimage for those who found its waters an ideal medicine for a great many ills.

It is said that the ghostly Abbess, head in hand, revisits the church and the well on certain nights of the year.

When the Devil Came to Danbury

The Bell is among the top twelve pub names found in England. Each has its own provenance and the reason behind its name. The Bell Inn, found in Danbury, is said to have taken its name from the place where the Devil dropped a stolen church bell.

The church in question is St John the Baptist where, legend has it, on Corpus Christie Day, which celebrates the eucharist in Christian religions, in 1402 the Devil made an appearance. As a huge storm raged outside, the Devil entered the church and behaved outrageously, frightening the congregation while the storm damaged the church roof and the chancel. Whereupon, pleased with his work, the Devil left the church.

He came back later, however, to steal one of the church's six bells. At which point the legend splits into two versions. One says the congregation chased him away and, as the bell became too heavy to carry, the Devil dropped it at a spot where its impact created a pond. The second version says he walked away unmolested, but the bell became too heavy to carry, so he dropped it at the spot where the Bell Inn now stands.

All of which of course is pure supposition, although it is said that today, the church has only five bells instead of the usual six.

The Bell Inn at Danbury.

Beauchamp Roding's Moving Stone

In the village of Beauchamp Roding, close to Chelmsford and one of eight local villages with the word Roding in their name, a large triangular-shaped bolder is buried in the grass of St Botolph's churchyard. Legend has it that the stone has been known to move up and down the hill on which the church is built. The stone was originally at the top of the hill, and was dragged downhill by villagers who wanted to use it in the construction of the church. But in the night, it moved up the hill again. After this had happened twice, the villagers gave up and built the church at the top of the hill. The stone originally lay flat on the ground, but in 1984, it was rolled into an upright position and half buried in the ground, where it can be seen today.

Old Harkilees

In Braintree Museum there is a large carved oak figure of an old man with a beard and long hair. It once stood in the village of Bocking on the corner of Bradford Street, then later was lifted to become part of the first-floor wall of a local alehouse. It is thought to date back to the seventeenth century, and some say it is an effigy of King Charles I.

The carving was known locally as Old Harkilees, possibly named after two tradesmen in the village, both named Hercules, a name which would sound more like 'harkilees' in the now forgotten accent of Essex people of the past.

For many years, village children were led to believe that the figure steps down from the wall and walks to the nearby river when the church bells strike midnight.

The Essex Gold Mines

Is it possible that gold was ever mined in Essex? Legend says that it might once have been the case around the villages of Little Thurrock, Orsett, East Tilbury and Chadwell St Mary. The story is derived from the mysterious shafts in this area driven into the ground and culminating in small caves. Their claim to being the lost gold mines of King Cunobelinus, one-time ruler of southern England, is more likely founded in the fact that Cunobelinus could have used the shafts and caves as a place to hide his hordes of gold.

Other stories claim that the shafts, known at one time as Dane Holes, were where local Saxons hid when the Danish Vikings invaded Essex. Likewise, they might have been used to excavate chalk for agricultural purposes in medieval times. Other claims include them being dwelling places, druid temples, smugglers' haunts, or traps for enemy invaders.

In the fourteenth century, King Henry IV commanded that the concealed gold mines should be investigated and anyone caught hiding them be brought before the king. In the fifteenth century, they were again rumoured to be gold mines and, for a while they were worked by miners who failed to find gold, but who did find outcrops of iron pyrite, a yellow mineral with a bright metallic lustre, often referred to as fool's gold, because of its resemblance to the real thing.

Like so many other myths, an element of truth such as this can sometimes mark the start of what eventually becomes a legend.

Picture Credits

Page 10: From *The Illustrated London News*, November 1861.
Page 15: Courtesy of the Creekmouth Preservation Society.
Page 14 (lower): From an unknown Victorian periodical.
Page 19: From a contemporary postcard.
Page 20 (right): By Daderot (public domain) via Wikimedia Commons.
Page 25 (right): Courtesy of Layer Marney Tower.
Page 26 (right): Courtesy of Mersea Museum/Carol Wyatt.
Page 27: From a contemporary postcard.
Page 29 (right); From the Wellcome Collection: Creative Commons license BY4.0.
Page 46 (right): From a contemporary postcard.
Page 48: By Steven Muster via Wikimedia Commons.
Page 55: Museo britannico del soprannaturale (public domain).
Page 67 (lower): © Acabashi, Creative Commons licence CC-BY-SA 4.0.
Page 68: By David Iliff. Creative Commons licence CC BY-SA 3.0.
Page 71: Genesisman26 at English Wikipedia (public domain).
Page 76 (top): Scott Wylie. Creative Commons licence CC BY 2.0.
Page 76 (lower): Mersea Museum/Len Harvey.
Page 77: Mersea Museum.
Page 80: From a contemporary post card.
Page 82: From a contemporary postcard.
Page 83: Courtesy of Martin Allen.
Page 85 (top): From a contemporary postcard.
Page 86 (top): From a contemporary postcard.

All other pictures by the author © John Wade

Index